WHERE THE BEAR
MET THE LION

WHERE THE BEAR MET THE LION

Afghanistan
1978-92

DR. KHALIL R. RAHMANY

authorHOUSE®

AuthorHouse™ LLC
1663 Liberty Drive
Bloomington, IN 47403
www.authorhouse.com
Phone: 1-800-839-8640

Published by AuthorHouse 01/29/2014

ISBN: 978-1-4918-5794-6 (sc)
ISBN: 978-1-4918-5793-9 (hc)
ISBN: 978-1-4918-5792-2 (e)

Library of Congress Control Number: 2014902005

For my brother Hafiz-u-Rahman

Contents

Preface

Writing a book about Afghanistan is not an easy task. To depict the war and its causes and implications, one should at least visit the battlefront. But crossing into Afghanistan is a risky business.

As an Afghan, I have not only seen the suffering in the war but have also been a victim. Early in 1979, my father; my brothers, Jamil-u-Rahman, Hafiz-u-Rahman, and Salim-u-Rahman; and I were imprisoned by the Soviet invaders. After six months, we all were released, except my youngest brother, Hafiz-u-Rahman. Later, we learned that he had been martyred by the ungodly Communists.

Such a fate befalls most Afghans who disagree with Communism and are unfortunate enough to be taken prisoner. The Soviets had no trials in Afghanistan.

My family, therefore, like millions of other innocent Afghans, chose to leave our home and our hearts and flee to Pakistan. There, I joined the resistance.

I witnessed several battles between the mujahideen and the Soviet invaders and later served for nearly three years as spokesman for the cause of my homeland's freedom war.

I came to understand the ominous threat the Soviet presence in Afghanistan posed to the security of South Asia and to world peace. I also witnessed the helplessness of most Western reporters, who longed for the truth and for eyewitness information but whose efforts were foiled.

Clearly advantaged by my experience, I decided to take the responsibility of presenting to the world a clear picture of the struggle in Afghanistan.

Dr. Khalil R. Rahmany

Accumulating the truth has been difficult; pursuing a single fact sometimes required weeks, months, or years. But persistence has been rewarded with unprecedented details of the savage cruelties inflicted on the innocent population, of the reaction and overwhelming protest of the free world against the Soviet invasion of nonaligned and independent nation, and of the heroic resistance of the Afghans and the bravery of a small nation that has never been subdued by any power except Allah

I am indebted to scores of people: Mujahideen commanders on the front, defected military officials, scholars, and resistance leaders in Peshawar, Pakistan, all generously contributed the vital information, intelligence reports, and most important, the personal knowledge and accounts contained in this book.

My thanks to my devoted family, who gave me full support and courage and guided me in my work.

My special thanks are due to my best friend, Mohammad Amin, who contributed long hours of editing and rewriting and used his expertise and skill, creativity, and imagination to weave a script that will be understood and appreciated by many.

Dr. Khalil R. Rahmany
New Year's Day 1992

Acknowledgments

The original manuscript was completed in 1992. Since then, the manuscript has been reviewed and revised by individuals familiar with the tragedy of the Afghan war.

First and foremost, I would like to express my gratitude to my dear friend Erin Speakman, who has invested his valuable time in reviewing and editing the manuscript. Erin's knowledge, perspicuity, and erudition in the domains of editing and awareness about the Afghan war have greatly contributed to the format and structure of the manuscript.

Second, I would like to express my appreciation to Ustad Saed, whose knowledge about the Afghan political turmoil and his insight about its historical significance has solidified the information provided in the manuscript. Ustad contributed long hours, reading the manuscript with careful and critical evaluation.

I am also in debt to scores of friends and colleagues, especially Dr. Howard Weisman, Dr. Meji Sigh, and Dr. Gilbert Weisman for their constant, generous support.

My special thanks goes to my dear family, Dr. Najib Rahmany, Doctoral Candidate Saema Rahmany, Khalid Rahmany, and Gulalai Rahmany, who have given me ongoing support and endurance and guided me in my work.

Thanks, Gulalai.
July 21, 2013

1

The Heritage

Long ago, in a time called prehistory, the ancestors of modern man roamed the earth, hunting great beasts and grubbing for roots.

Embryonic clans wandered the endless, lonely world for countless millennia—memories of past, of origins, faded forever.

A few, perhaps, walked the high place of desert and forest and mountains, where three vast continents converged, the place of the ibex, arid bear, and tiger.

Thousands of years of wanderers had passed when one small migratory clan ended its ancient journey here in Neolithic times. Settlement had quietly come to the land we now call Afghanistan.

Other settlements, based on domesticated animals and crude agriculture, appeared and developed in the fertile valleys along the lower slopes of the harsh mountain ranges and along the ancient Oxus River.

With the coming of the Bronze Age, the inhabitants embarked on—and sometimes received—daring trading expeditions by which the Afghan commodity, a semi-precious blue stone called lapis lazuli, found its way to the advanced civilizations of the Indus Valley Harappa, Babylonian Mesopotamia, and even the isolated early dynastic Egypt; before the first pyramid arose, Afghan lapis lazuli was there.

Regardless, the place from which the stone came was practically unknown to the outside world. What is probably a reference to the region appears in a prototype of the Rig-Veda, the earliest known Hindu scriptures, which could date back to 2000 BC, but the reference is sketchy at best. The enigmatic passage breathes of a descent upon the Indian subcontinent from Central Asia. The fathers of the Sanskrit canticles, spells, and rituals that would become the Vedic literature were Aryan, a name encompassing the entire Indo-European race and language family, whose deepest roots are among the semi-nomads of Transcaucasia and the Afghan plateau. The verses of the first Indians mention only fleetingly the place of their ancestors.

A later, slightly more detailed reference appears in an ancient Indo-Greek script, believed to have been written by Herodotus in 1500 BC, though there is no indication that the Greeks knew of their own Aryan ancestry. The name "Bactria" is first used here, which refers to the semi-arid steppe between the Oxus and the north flank of the Hindu Kush, the name given to the mountains that split Afghanistan. Also described is a thriving city in the wilderness south of Bactria, the primeval city called Kubaha, which, quite probably, may have evolved into modern-day Kabul.

Afghanistan in those days was known to the outside world as little more than a rugged, troublesome trade route between the Mediterranean and the Far Orient, a geographical obstacle to overcome. And for a thousand years, even that image was almost exclusive to the painfully infrequent caravan merchants and the few who would hear their tales. While magnificent kingdoms advanced and crumbled, while glorious dynasties flourished and died away, the high plateau sustained a shroud of irrelevance and utter remoteness.

Finally, in the sixth century BC, the region achieved historical significance when the Persian Achaemenid conqueror Cyrus the Great thought enough of the land to seize it and its sparse population as part of a very memorable empire that dominated the "civilized" world from Libya to Transcaucasia to India.

Roughly two hundred years later, the immortalized Macedonian, Alexander the Great, swept across Asia Minor and defeated the armies of Darius III, a successor of Cyrus, and then turned his own armies eastward, toward the riches of India. On a grand campaign of conquest, the Afghan plateau was merely consequential, although it was here, in the Pamir Mountains, that Alexander found a wife, Roxana.

It is believed that Alexander knew of and used the Khyber Pass and the narrower Malakand Pass to invade India. For centuries to follow, invading armies from either direction would recognize the strategic importance of the Khyber (a rugged crack in the mountainous barrier that, coupled with the untamed deserts of Baluchistan in the south, geographically isolates India from the west). The Khyber, always remembered in the legends of the merchants of antiquity, has been both a blessing and a curse to the peoples of the plateau.

The Greeks ultimately receded, but they left behind an outpost city and a heritage. Even today, much of Afghanistan architecture, custom, and even genetic origin is a legacy of the Greco-Bactrian period.

This would be an ongoing element of Afghanistan's cultural evolvement. Centuries upon centuries of invasion by military exoduses from every direction would create a mosaic society of unparalleled color.

Displacing the Greeks was a confederation of Scythian-related nomadic tribes called Yueh-chih, who had migrated from the Kashgar area of Chinese Turkestan to establish their Kushan Empire, of which Bactria became a desirable part. The Yueh-chih brought with them Gandhara-style Buddhism and its notable art form, as well as an appreciation of exotic goods from faraway places. Very commerce-minded, the Kushans were able to obtain their foreign treasures by allowing, even advocating, a vital link of the imperial silk route to exist in Afghanistan, as well as further north in Turkestan. Merchants from an emerging Rome, from China, and from India all rendezvoused at caravansaries in Afghanistan.

Kushan strength was short-lived, however, and for centuries past anno Domini, Central Asian territory would be wrestled between the warlords of Persia, Parthia, Anatolia, Turkestan, and even the Huns of the far north. The golden age of the exchange of wares and ideas between East and West was slain by the ruthlessness of kingdoms and men. Trade was frozen, and the Silk Road, for a time, vanished.

It was a dark period.

Under God, Judaism had been scattered to the ends of the earth. Christianity had been exiled by the fiercely corrupt of a fallen Rome.

Finally, near the end of the sixth century after Jesus, there came for the people of the land a final prophet. The distant sands of Arabia saw the birth of the messenger, Muhammad (peace be upon him) and the word of Allah) was carried forth on the mediums of war and later on its vestiges. From a dim cave in a mountain-locked hamlet called Mecca, the message, in a single generation, reached the continents of Africa, Europe, and Asia. Its gateway to Asia was, naturally, the Afghan plateau, and it

3

was here that Islam found a people that would become among its most dedicated followers.

Paganism fled. Buddhism and Hinduism retreated. Even the pre-Achaemenid native religion of Zoroastrianism, considered a predecessor of the Muslim belief, bowed to the swell of Islam. It was a time of religious awakening, unprecedented in that part of the world, and the words of the Quran came to be perhaps the greatest influence of all upon the Afghan people and what was to be their nation. So profound was the effect upon their laws, customs, morality, and government that the history of Islam is, in a sense, the history of the Afghans.

These were the Middle Ages. Eurasian civilization had shifted dramatically. While most of Europe staggered blindly through its dark age, the rising Muslim world entered a classical period. Alexandria and Baghdad became the intellectual centers of the world, and their Central Asian satellites, Bukhara, Samarkand, and Balkh, basked in brilliance.

The nearby city of Ghazni also prospered when it became the capital of a magnificent empire that spanned from Persia well into India. The empire reached the apex of its advance during the rule of the sultan Mahmud Ghaznavi but continued to grow when the Ghaznavis were succeeded by the Khwarezms.

Suddenly, in 1216, the civilization was overwhelmed by the mounted hordes of a savage conqueror from Mongolia, whose name, even today, causes a shudder in the hearts of those whose ancestors fell to him: the terrible Genghis Khan. Scores of Asian cities were plundered and left in ruin. As the Khwarezms escaped to the distant Caspian Sea, the resplendent cities of Bamian, Herat, Ghazni, and Balkh were virtually destroyed. It seemed the Middle Ages had run its course. Just as the people of the plateau had been razed and left in devastation, Europe was experiencing a Renaissance, and China was again looking westward. The death of Genghis Khan left no united power in Central Asia, and so, after centuries of abandon, the Silk Route of old again felt the footsteps of East-West trade. A few decades after Genghis's barbaric scourge, the storied Venetian explorer Marco Polo, en route to the Kublai Khan's palace in Cathay, arrived with his uncle's in Balkh. Among the oldest cities in Asia, Balkh was once known by the Arabs as the "Mother of Cities," an exquisite, fortified trace of civilization in the high desert. Marco found it an uninhabited, blackened ruin of crumbled mosque and palace. Not all the region was destitute, however, and Marco's expedition is reputed to have stayed a full year in an agreeable Badakhshan, a few days east of Balkh.

Conclusive recovery came late in the fourteenth century by the unlikely means of a second Tartar-Mongol invasion. Emerging from the city of Samarkand, Timor the Lame ("Tamerlane" to Europeans) stormed across Eurasia in the grand style of Genghis Khan before him, leaving in his wake heaps of rubble and towers of skulls. Timor's vandal hordes penetrated as far west as Byzantium and the Sahara, as far north as Moscow, and as far east as Delhi, from which he exported elephants back to Samarkand for the arduous undertaking of erecting the magnificent structures that would make Samarkand the jewel of Asia. Also delivered to Central Asia were the scholars and artisans of the kingdoms Timor defeated.

As a result, the Timurid Dynasty following Timor's death became the renaissance of the plateau and was a time of enlightenment, revival, and peace. When the dynasty effectively came to an end in the early sixteenth century, an Uzbek tribesman called Babur, who claimed descendance from Genghis and Timor, gained control of the region, making Kabul the seat of his principality. Following the conquest of the Delhi sultanate, ruled by the last Afghan sultan over India, Babur's capital was moved to Agra in the year 1526, and the Mughal Empire was created. The empire would see its most glorious years under Babur's grandson, Akbar.

But the high plateau would not share in the glory. The gravity of India's charm made Afghanistan rather inconspicuous in comparison, and the region soon drifted well outside Mughal interest.

For two hundred years, tribal khans lorded over local areas, while a very lax claim to territory divided the Mughals and the Persians, if only in theory.

Finally, after decades of isolated uprisings against Persian dominance, which had remained significant, the Ottoman Empire invaded Persia from the west, and a band of Afghans overran the capital of Esfahan in the east. The instability promised to reach crisis proportions, so a Turkmen Afghan named Nader advanced from the north to reunite the kingdom. He was remarkably successful and within years achieved the title of shah.

After pacifying the Ottomans, Nader Shah turned an army of kinsmen and Persians against the Mughals, yet with apparently no intention of supplanting the rulers. Having seized the treasures of Delhi and Agra, the shah returned to Persia, leaving the Mughals to contend with the simpler problems of recent French and British colonialism of India.

Nader was assassinated by his subjects in 1747.

Eventually, all the Afghan commanders left the country. Persia was returned to the Persians.

One former commander, a Pashtun called Ahmad Shah Abdali Durrani, decided to return to his birthplace, the high plateau, where tribal khans lorded over local areas as they had for centuries. In Ahmad Shah Abdali Durrani, the Afghan tribes at last found a ruler, and for the first time, the ancient mountain people who had lived on the land since the beginning of history stood and claimed their motherland and their right to self-determination. The mosaic of peoples who shared a common heritage, united under one of their own, and Ahmad Abdali was, from that day onward, Ahmad Sha Baba—Ahmad Shah, our father. There was born on that day the kingdom of Afghanistan, land of the Afghans.

2

Genesis of a Modern World

The death of Ahmad Shah in 1772 plunged the young nation into disarray. Though sons and grandsons tried to assume inherited rule, the transient lineage of kings was ignored by the stoutly autocratic Afghan tribes.

Finally, in 1826, an Afghan named Dost Mohammad won recognition as amir, the accepted ruler over the Afghan khanates. Fortunate was this granting of power, for it was under Dost Mohammad that the sovereign of Afghanistan would first be challenged.

At this time, two great empires had rushed upon the borders of Afghanistan. In the north, Czar Alexander I, encouraged by his ally Napoleon Bonaparte, had marched the armies of Russia into the Muslim regions of Central Asia. Only the Emirate of Bukhara successfully resisted conquest and presently distracted the Czar's rampage south toward India.

In the south and the east, the British Empire had triumphed over France in total colonization of India and now stood impatient at its mountainous western extremity, where a tribal army held them in check at the Khyber Pass.

Of the two empires encroaching intentions, it was England's colonial ambitions that proved the most immediate threat. Although it may be that Britain was provoked because it believed that Dost Mohammad sought Russian assistance to liberate Peshawar (an Indian border town) from the Sikhs (the fierce Muslim-Hindu syncretism with whom Britain had allied), it is far more likely that the czar's aggression compelled the British to try to seize Afghanistan before rival Russia could. In any case, the British East India Company in 1839 attacked the Khyber Pass with force. The outgunned Afghan tribesmen were overrun.

In April, Kandahar was captured; the following July, Ghazni. In August, Kabul was occupied, and the British army placed on the throne Shah Shuja, the unpopular Afghan whom Dost Mohammad had ousted. Dost Mohammad was now exiled.

Victory was fleeting, however. The aristocratic arrogance of the British toward their conquered subjects evoked a massive rebellion. Hundreds of British and Indian troops were massacred in the valleys of Kandahar and Kabul. Much of Kabul was burned to the ground, a sacrifice preferable to subjugation. The Afghans retook the land. Their Amir Dost Mohammad, returned.

Twenty years later, the Amir's third son, Sher Ali, inherited Kabul. In 1878, the new Amir invited a Russian envoy but denied British missionaries entry into Afghanistan. This, of course, angered the British, and the Anglo-Indian forces again invaded, taking Kabul in 1879. Sher Ali was driven from the capital and, weeks later, died in Mazar-i-Sharif in northern Afghanistan.

Though decades had strengthened the British army since the last fated occupation of Afghanistan, the British Parliament nonetheless would now seek friendly cooperation with the Afghans. Sher Ali's son, Yaqub Khan, was granted his father's throne and, in mutual respect, signed with the British the Treaty of Gandamak, which gave the Afghans full domestic sovereignty and gave the British an embassy in Kabul. Although the treaty, perceived as obligatory by Yaqub Khan, gave Britain legal authority over Afghanistan's foreign policy, this authority, in practice, would be idle. Yaqub and his successor would continue to manage all policies, and the treaty would simply assure Russia that an act of ambition against Afghanistan would be met by the British army.

Yaqub Khan would not long rule. British arrogance had not been forgotten, and British/tribal conflicts again erupted, and Yaqub Khan fled. When Britain finally withdrew, a cousin of Sher Ali, Abdurrahman Khan, assumed rulership.

Abdurrahman's legacy would be the modern borders of Afghanistan, the products so vital to powerful nations and so meaningless to the Afghans and their ancient neighbors, yet necessary to Abdurrahman, who daily confronted the surges of a modern world that would loom ever nearer. The Oxus River and the peaks of the Pamir would serve as the border with Russia. An imperceptible boundary would be drawn in the east and the south. In 1893, the Treaty of Durand was signed, and the border, the Durand Line, was declared, splitting the Khyber Pass, placing Peshawar permanently outside Kabul's influence and politically dividing many tribes. These tribes, once unalterably connected, have since evolved culturally on opposite sides of a border and today commonly have separate names: the Pashtuns of Afghanistan and the Pathans of Pakistan (former West India).

Abdurrahman's domestic success was prouder. His swelling army eventually balanced the might of the tribal chieftains, encouraging peaceful community between tribe and central government and bringing a more significant sense of national unity to the diverse peoples of Afghanistan.

Abdurrahman died with the nineteenth century. As the early rays of morning fall on a man lost in a cold desert night, bringing light and warmth yet a fearful destiny, so too dawned the twentieth century, bringing hope and growth and movement, companions to the awesome promise of fate—the fate inevitable when ideas, near and far, collide.

Abdurrahman's son and successor, Habibullah, inherited a worldlier Afghanistan. His era began in 1901 and would be devoted to the maintenance of Abdurrahman's foreign policy. The opposing forces of Russia and British India would be buffered by Afghanistan, and the power of both would be balanced, one against the other, to preserve the independence of the vulnerable Afghan state.

Domestically, Habibullah's main concern was uncertainty. International awareness was emerging in Kabul and other cities, and the influence on the culture was unsettling. The ultimate course of this new internationalism was, of course, hardly predictable, but a rising dissatisfaction in the younger generation was apparent in Habibullah's own son, Amanullah, who was never without a complaint about his father's traditional way of government.

Worldwide, the factories, railroads, and other technologies of the nineteenth century had intimately connected unsuspecting nations on every continent. Trade had evolved into the framework of what would become a global economy. Interests of nations once separated by geography and culture were now interdependent. A quarrel between two nations suddenly involved many nations.

In 1914, World War I was declared. Amanullah beseeched his father to align with the central empires (Germany, Austria-Hungary, Bulgaria, and the Ottomans), who would be eager to invade India and crush British colonialism there. Amir Habibullah refused, probably for fear of an unbalanced Russian power.

In 1918, World War I was over. The next year, Habibullah was assassinated, most likely by his impatient son, who ascended the throne and resolved to eradicate Afghanistan.

Meanwhile, the oppressed peasants of Russia, spirited by the writings of a man named Karl Marx, had risen in the Great October Revolution, overthrown the last residues of the ancient czardom, and placed three revolutionaries—Vladimir Lenin, Leon Trotsky, and Josef Stalin—in power. In the midst of trying to crush a civil rebellion by the anti-Communist White Army, Lenin received a letter from Amanullah Khan, extending preliminary recognition of Lenin's regime and inviting friendly relations with Afghanistan. On May 27, Lenin sent a positive response to Kabul. Within hours, Amanullah, assured of no threat from Russia, denounced the Treaty of Gandamak and declared war on British India and its presence in Afghanistan.

The colonial power, weakened by growing Indian resistance and especially by World War I, was insufficient to resist expulsion by fierce Afghan warriors. It was the last British-Afghan war.

In August of 1919, Afghan delegates were received into India to negotiate a treaty. The Treaty of Rawalpindi officially recognized the full sovereignty of the nation of Afghanistan and subsequently by the European nations and the rest of the world. Heralding the decline of Britain's colonial strength, the treaty became an icon of hope to those Indians who dreamed of independence.

In February 1921, Amanullah and Lenin concluded a treaty of friendship and mutual cooperation. The same year, the White Army was defeated, and the united Communist state was born. In 1922, the Union of Soviet Socialist Republics was established.

Though a reactive insurrection was rising in the Central Asian republics that had been seized by the czar and were now being invaded by Communism, the main threat to Communist Moscow fell with the defeat of the White Army and the firmly entrenched Soviets were now able to send a wealth of resources to Afghanistan.

Kabul received an influx of envoys, economic aid, and armaments, as well as a number of technical and military advisors to train the Afghan army and royal air force.

Moscow struggled to build a bridge of trust with Afghanistan, even promising the return of Panjda and Marwa, two northern areas seized from Amir Dost Mohammad during the czarist military adventures in Central Asia.

Well into the 1920s, however, Moscow continued to tighten her grasp on all her outpost territories, including Panjda and Marwa. In fact, the Emirate of Bukhara was fighting a fierce but losing battle against Soviet annexation. The resistance would continue to struggle until 1928, when Bukhara would finally be absorbed into the surrounding Soviet republics of Uzbekistan, Turkmenia, and Tajikistan.

Cultural and religious ties with the invaded peoples of Central Asia forced the Afghan masses to receive and support the refugees, who fled to Afghanistan by the thousands. Even the amir of Bukhara, Syed Aleem Khan, fled his fallen kingdom to die as a refugee in the foreign land of Afghanistan.

Hundreds of thousands died in the struggle to defend their homeland and their Islamic ways, believing that a socialist form of government would undermine and obliterate the traditions of Bukhara. This belief was not unfounded. The society imposed on the Muslims of the surrounding Soviet republics illustrated clearly the ways that Communism conflicts with Islam. Indeed, no fewer than twenty-five thousand mosques had been leveled since the Soviet move into Central Asia.

Many Afghans began to ponder the fate of Bukhara and wondered if Soviet influence in Kabul might lead to similar aggression in Afghanistan.

While the Soviets pressured Kabul to hand over the Bukharian refugees as criminals of war, Amanullah Khan was being pressured by strong and widespread public opinion to expel all Soviet envoys and advisors from Afghanistan.

Unwillingly, Amanullah finally submitted to the demands of his people and severed relations with the Soviet Union. Not surprisingly, the British arrived to fill the diplomatic vacuum. This time, they were not feared. The Treaty of Rawalpindi and Britain's fading power in India were insurance enough that England would not again pursue colonial power in Afghanistan.

Though Afghanistan had supported the Bukharan resistance, there stirred in the mind of Amanullah Khan the same liberal ideologies the Bukhara were resisting. Amanullah had traveled extensively, visiting the Soviet Union, England, France, Italy, Egypt, Turkey, Iran (modern Persia), and India. Returning to Afghanistan, he had brought with him many foreign ideas. In 1926, he replaced his title of amir with the title of shah. Soon, Shah Amanullah Khan was calling for liberal reforms of the Afghan Constitution. For instance, the traditional law of purdah (the veiling of women) was denounced, and the introduction of European dress was ordered.

When Amanullah's wife, Queen Soraya, appeared at Parliament without her veil, the spark of insurrection ignited throughout the country. The Afghan people received the act as a serious insult to their tradition and the integrity of the nation.

Amanullah's actions, in the opinion of his subjects, were comparable to the secular policies of Mustafa Kemal Ataturk, who, as present ruler of Turkey, was effecting the fall of the Ottoman sultanate and introducing, in its place, Western republicanism, Roman rather than Arabic script, and the elimination of Islam from government and law. Though generally popular in Turkey, a society lacking religious unity and desiring modernization, the same reforms thrust upon Afghanistan, a traditional society, unified by Islam, could only be met with rebellion.

In 1929, Amanullah, growing steadily aware of the unrest of his people, withdrew some of his reforms and diplomatically called on nearly a thousand religious scholars and tribal leaders to reconcile their opposition to him.

It was too late. The nation called him "against Islam and against Afghanistan." Ulema and chieftains throughout the country converged in mosques and councils, and jihad, or holy war, was ordered against Amanullah's regime.

The deposed king abdicated and fled Afghanistan, eventually finding asylum in Italy, where he would later die.

The Soviets impetuously accused India's British Raj of fueling the fire of insurgence against Amanullah. The Soviets have also blamed Amanullahor not bringing land reform to Afghanistan. They had promoted land reform in a country in which 85 percent of the citizens were farmers, saying that this would effect change in the social order and secure peace. In reality, it was that sort of revolutionary thinking that brought Amanullah's downfall.

Unfortunately, due to poor communications between tribes, it was an unorganized rebellion with no provision for who would replace Amanullah. Consequently, a Tajik peasant called Bach-i-Saqao assumed control and governed Kabul for nine months, while the rest of the country was left in anarchy.

The British, fearful the Soviets might march across the lawless Hindu Kush and Nuristan to challenge the British-Indian border, invited Mohammad Nader (formerly a general under Amanullah who had retired to France because of policy disagreements with the shah) to return to the subcontinent and restore order to the buffer state. Nader, assisted by British troops and a Ghilzai Pashtun tribal confederation, stormed Kabul and seized power. Bachi Saqua was driven from the city and later killed.

The new khan, though in favor of progress and having the resources, was able to accomplish little during his brief reign. In his steps to construct a more democratic government, he was elected to the *Walase Jirga*, or House of the People, an exclusive cabinet of landlords and tribal leaders. In 1931, he initiated a constitutional form of law. Later, he raised a new army of twelve thousand Afghan troops. Then, in 1933, while receiving the graduates of a military school, Nader Khan was assassinated by an armed student, whose father, a militant supporter of Amanullah, had been executed in the early months of Nader Khan's regime. The brutal punishment inflicted upon the assassin continued for days until he was finally stoned down on a public avenue.

Mohammad Zahir Shah was nineteen years old when he was placed on the throne of Afghanistan. For the following two decades, he lazily sat as ruler while three other members of the royal Mohammadzai family actually governed the nation. Prime Minister Hashem khandirected covertly until 1946, Afterwards Prime Minister Shah Mahmoud ran the government, who was subsequently replaced by Marshal Shah Wali Khan, who has taken charge of the governemtn untile 1953. During the course of these years Zahir's title of king essentially became cosmetic.

In the 1930s, the young regime was primarily occupied with a host of internationally sponsored development projects. It was a time of unprecedented cultural contradictions. At the same time that Zahir Shah's family was taking steps to bring tradition back to Afghanistan, influences from all over the world dominated the commercial sector.

Furthermore, these development projects themselves contrasted the actual world situation. While diplomats from most of the world's developed nations cooperated on the remote plateau of Afghanistan, their mother countries tottered on the brink of global conflict.

In Europe, Adolf Hitler, with the help of Benito Mussolini, began expanding the great German state into Poland, Austria, and Czechoslovakia. In northeast Asia, the Japanese emperor began the invasion of Manchuria.

The year 1939 arrived, and World War II exploded in Europe, North Africa, the Far East, and the South Pacific. The Axis forces moved against Great Britain and the Soviet Union. Japan signed a treaty with Hitler. The United States of America aligned with Western Europe, the Soviet Union, and China, clashing with Nazism/Fascism on every continent of the Eastern Hemisphere.

Afghanistan, meanwhile, faced a serious dilemma. While the Japanese hastened to the Pacific to support their motherland, the remaining German and Italian advisors were interned in Kabul at the insistence of Allied representatives in Afghanistan. This action, forced by threats of severed diplomacy from the Allied nations, threatened to weaken the Kabul government's ties to nonalignment and neutrality, a policy that had meant the survival of Afghan independence for centuries.

Kabul nervously waited for the end of the war. If the Allied nations were to be victorious, perhaps they would remain allies, meaning the end of Afghanistan's value as a buffer state and, perhaps, ultimately her subjugation by the united powers of Great Britain and the Soviet Union. If the Axis forces were to be victorious and Hitler's master plan executed, Afghanistan would certainly fade into a global dictatorship. The more likely possibility was that Hitler would be defeated, the Western-Asian alliance would disband and realign politically and economically, much in the manner as before the war, and Afghanistan could again balance Great Britain against the Soviet Union.

As the war raged on, however, England suffered greatly, as did her colonial interests abroad. The viceroy of India declared a state of war against the Fascist powers and began flying supplies to China over the Himalayan spine, to the discomfort of Indian nationals who feared the Japanese might invade from Burma at any moment. Clamors for independence from Britain rang louder than ever. Mahatma Gandhi launched his civil disobedience campaign. The Muslim League insisted on an independent state of Pakistan, presuming an end to the Commonwealth's hold on India; England was losing power.

In the spring of 1945, Berlin fell, and Hitler took his own life. The following summer, the United States exploded its first offensive atomic bombs on Hiroshima and Nagasaki, and Japan surrendered.

The Soviet Union emerged as the greatest power in Europe and Asia. Great Britain emerged somewhat crippled. Fortunately, the new strength of the United States could rival that of the Soviets, and Kabul was able to construct a delicate balance based on the continued development of Afghanistan.

In 1946, Zahir Shah's government made an agreement with Washington, DC, and American firms—most prominently, the Morrison Knudsen Corporation—began a new series of projects, beginning with the irrigation of hundreds of hectometers of wasteland in the Helmand Valley. In the following months, the United States constructed Kandahar International Airport and carved the road connecting Kabul with Islam Qalah, the border town en route to Iran's Mashhad Province.

Meanwhile, Soviet workers built an air base in Bagram and forged a road connecting Kabul with the northern village of Shabarghan, as well as contracting the Nangarhar water and power project and Ghazi's Sarda Irrigation Project and building a fertilizer factory in Mazar-i-Sharif. The international activity in Afghanistan accelerated during the next few years, a time of great political change in South Asia.

In August 1947, the British Commonwealth and Her Majesty's army, guided by Lord Mountbatten, seceded from India. Simultaneously, the Punjabi and Bengali "wings" of India partitioned to form the anticipated independent state of Pakistan.

Fortunately—and not a moment too soon—Afghanistan had become a diplomatic crossroads. Furthermore, the United States had intervened militarily on the subcontinent. While not replacing Britain as a protectorate of Afghanistan, Washington did vow to build up the military of Pakistan, placing the Afghan-Pak border within the Western realm of interest. The following year, the imminent Cold War erupted across the globe, and the new socialism versus capitalism posture became assurance enough that the United States would not wish for Communism to sweep across the Pakistani border.

A new, temporarily secure balance of power was established. Kabul had grasped the challenges of World War II and had not merely survived but profited in it.

In its proud success, however, the regime became somewhat precipitous. By 1950, 55 percent of Afghanistan's treaties were with the Soviet Union, outweighing all other treaties combined. Since no immediate threat from Pakistan existed, it was a precarious imbalance, though perceived by Kabul as a necessity toward further economic development, as resources shipped over the border from the Soviet Union were far less expensive than resources freighted over ten thousand miles from the United States. Additionally, the United States refused to aid Afghanistan militarily, as it might conflict with American military interests in Pakistan, a nation half expecting a war with Afghanistan over the status of the Pathan tribes living in the hills between the Indus River and the Afghan border.

The new reliance on the USSR resulted in Soviet influence in Afghanistan that was comparable to that invited by Amanullah Khan in the early 1920s. Hundreds of Soviet doctors, engineers, and military advisors were assigned to Afghanistan, each with instructions to weave Marxist/Leninist philosophy into the nation's professional class. Anti-Western sentiments began to fester among young Afghan students and military officers. In Kabul and Kandahar, there arose an idea that the United States and Pakistan conspired to deny liberty to the Pathan tribesman of Pakistan. The Cold War flared throughout Afghanistan. The Soviets were winning.

In 1953, Zahir Shah's cousin, the Soviet-educated Mohammad Daoud, was appointed prime minister of Afghanistan. Virtually all the king's power was entrusted to Daoud, though the power to dismiss him, fortunately, remained with Zahir.

Josef Stalin died that year. The Soviet Presidium, though in crisis, maintained a political stronghold in Afghanistan, with the cooperation of Daoud.

Daoud adopted an oppressive and contradictory policy of government, denying any political expression by the Afghan people except on the issue of "Pashtunistan," for which he encouraged political activism.

The "Pashtunistan" movement, led by a Pathan, Abdul Ghafar Khan, was initiated in response to Pakistan's partition from India. The movement pressed for a second division that would form an independent state stretching from the Indus River to the Afghan border. The new state would be ruled in the same tribal manner as Afghanistan, with whom it would be closely affiliated, as Afghanistan, after all, was ruled by Pashtuns.

It was suspected by the people of Afghanistan that Daoud's obsession with Pashtunistan was little more than a yearning for an outlet to the Arabian Sea and its respective trade routes.

The cause of Pashtunistan nonetheless was supported by the Afghan people on the grounds that it was what their kinsmen in Pakistan wanted. \

In 1955, while Daoud was visiting the Kremlin (Soviet Assembly Headquarters), Pakistan, supported by the Southeast Asia Treaty Organization (SEATO), declared the unity of West Pakistan, officially denouncing the validity of Abdul Ghafar Khan's partition movement. Tensions erupted, Daoud hastily returned to post, and Kabul began mobilizing her armed forces along the Durand Line, while Pakistan simultaneously evacuated her citizens from Afghanistan and blockaded the mouth of the Khyber Pass at Landi Kotal. The Soviet Union officially withdrew recognition of the Pakistan government. Soviet Premier Nikolai Bulganin and his first secretary, Nikita Khrushchev, arrived in Kabul with a ten-year lease of $100 million.

The following year, SEATO, of which the United States, France, and several Commonwealth nations were members, held a conference in Karachi. The organization announced to the world press its unanimous opposition to the partition of a separate Pashtunistan.

This infuriated Daoud, and an additional $25 million lease agreement was signed with the Soviet Union. The other members of the royal family, however, growing increasingly wary of the new role of the USSR, a sole source of trade, pressured Daoud to ease relations with Pakistan. He agreed to some scanty trade concessions with Karachi but continued to concur with Moscow's infiltration of virtually all aspects of Afghan life.

Hundreds of youths from the Afghan countryside were sent to the cosmopolitan centers of the Soviet Union to be educated in secular universities. Those students who declined the non-Islamic education were returned to Afghanistan in disgrace. Those who submitted were instructed in advanced topics, each with an underlying element of Marxist thought. Many were taught the benefits of Communism. All lived in unaccustomed luxury, surrounded by easily accessed vodka and unveiled girls. Upon graduation, these youths were sent back to their homeland, disillusioned with its archaic economy and culture.

Daoud replaced much of his cabinet with these new, innovative elite. Clamor for modernization reverberated through Afghanistan's urban areas. Before the close of this first Daoud era, a significant percentage of Afghanistan's rising generation had some form of Soviet education. This recent wave of Soviet influence reached its zenith following another crippling blow to Afghan-Pakistani relations over the issue of Pashtunistan.

In 1960, Daoud's most recent collaborator in the movement, the Pakistani fakir of IPI, died. The following autumn, Kabul supported a rash Mohammed tribal invasion of Pakistan's remote frontier territory of Din. An independent-minded feudal chieftain in the area, the khan of Khar, successfully fell upon the invaders, who, after considerable casualties, finally retreated to the wild hills of the Malakand Pass. Pakistan learned of Kabul's involvement and was infuriated.

By the beginning of 1961, embassies were closed in Karachi and Kabul, and all friendly relations ceased.

For Afghanistan, the following twenty months was a time of multitudinous dealings with the Communist world. Kabul received Czechoslovakian-built MiG fighter aircraft, Soviet tanks, and a vast arsenal of light arms and ammunition. Although the Sino-Soviet split had begun, the Afghan monarchy even secured trade agreements with Communist China, with whom Afghanistan shares a common fifty miles of border at the far end of the Wakhan Corridor.

Finally, in 1963, Mohammed Reza Pahlavi, shah of Iran, intervened in the diplomatic crisis between his neighbors. His patient mediation led to the reopening of trade offices between Afghanistan and Pakistan.

A more significant result was Zahir Shah's dismissal of Daoud in the interest of friendship with Pakistan. The action was popular among Afghans as well as the European circulesEven Soviet-educated Afghans who were given high posts in the administration and felt oppressed by Daoud, have celebrated the dissmimal.

Zahir Shah began a decade of experimental Western-style democracy, which partially offset the Communist influence in the country.

Nonetheless, the seeds of Marxism had taken root in the land of the Afghans.

3

The Intrigues of Daoud

King Zahir's democratic policies included freedom of the press and the freedom to form political parties. This opened the doors, ironically, to the formation of the People's Democratic Party of Afghanistan (PDPA) on January 1, 1965, the nation's first official Communist organization. The founders of the party were Noor Mohammad Taraki, a Ghalji Pashtun, was a veteran of the raisin business. The Kandahar-based company he worked for had sent him, as a young man, to India, where he was exposed to Marxist philosophy by the Communist Party in Bombay. Later, the Afghan government sent Taraki—although his education was scant—to work the embassy in Washington, DC, where he openly criticized the policies of Mohammed Daoud, who was, at that time, prime minister. Regardless, Taraki's return home was unpunished, and he was given a job as translator at the American embassy in Kabul, a fact that would later be held against him.

Babrak, an upper-class Tajik, was born and raised in the city. As the son of a general, Babrak was close to the royal family and indeed was treated as a family member on his frequent visits to the palace. Conversely, Babrak's visits to the Soviet embassy in Kabul were equally frequent; he quite probably was an agent of the KGB (the Soviet secret service).

Another man, Hafizullah Amin, became associated with the founders because of his significance in the growth of the party. Amin, like Taraki, had spent time in the United States, where he had great

20

success at Columbia University. Surprisingly, it was in America that Amin found and became infatuated with Communism. Amin was of a calm nature. Only the very perceptive might sense the darker temperament that waited within him. The party printed its first newspaper, *Khalq* (which means "people"), in 1966. The front page was strewn with words of the Great October Bolshevik Revolution and slogans calling for proletarian international solidarity. Though the words were strange and unfamiliar to most of the Afghan peasantry, the educated recognized a call to the rise of the oppressed class (to which most Afghans claimed membership), the seizure of the nation's means of production, and the abolishment of the aristocracy. This message was, of course, quite subtle but nonetheless clear to all those with a Marxist education—or any academic education, for that matter. The king, however, apparently accepted the words as symbolic of an ideal, rather than an entreaty to action, for his cooperation with the PDPA was entire.

Khalq spawned a reactionary movement that began, primarily, with the latest generation of students at Kabul University, who organized an on-campus demonstration for October 25. As students peacefully protested Communist activism, as well as the increasing autocracy of the king, a police unit, under the orders of Abdul Mali, son-in-law of Zahir, arrived at the university and opened machine-gun fire. Seventeen students were killed.

The citizens of Kabul were outraged. In defiance, more demonstrations proceeded, even in the high schools. For years to follow, on October 25, students would demonstrate in recognition of *Shohada*, or Day of the Martyrs.

The incident in 1966 sharply divided the university. Established rivalries escalated as pro-Communists clashed with anti-Communists in the halls. On the left, students and faculty members claimed membership in the PDPA or in a Maoist group, the Shughla-i-Jaweed ("Eternal Light"). An incidental nationalist group wanted Ataturkian Western democracy. On the right, Islamic activist called themselves the *Betaraf,* or the "Neutral Ones."

Meanwhile, the PDPA, still in its infancy, was suffering an inner turmoil that undermined Islamic opposition (which was viewed as obscure by PDPA's leadership anyway). By 1967, the party that preached solidarity was breaking apart. It splintered, and two major factions emerged: Khalq, led by Taraki, and Parcham, led by Babrak. The split was a result of policy disagreements, as well as racial and personal differences.

Parcham, the new faction's newspaper—which called King Zahir a "wise and progressive ruler" and was incidentally most closely affiliated with Moscow—was allowed to publish. Khalq, which neglected to display friendliness to the king, was banned in the midst of Zahir's decomposing democracy.

Taraki, with complete disaffection, called *Parcham* the "Royal Communist Party," a title Babrak proudly accepted.

The following year, a Sharia-law student, Abdu Rahim Niazi, held a meeting of YoungMuslims at Kabul University. Communism and the kingdom of Zahir Shah was the topic. The conference eventually turned to a recollection of a man called Sayed Jamaluddin Afghan, who in 1885 brought unity to the various tribes under the Banner of Islam. This unity had led, ultimately, to the expulsion of the British occupation forces blocking the independence of Afghanistan.

By evening's end, the loosely associated Young Muslim decided to unite under the name of Nau Jawanan-i-Muslman, and the Muslim Youth Organization (MYO) was formed.

Led by a panel of students and professors, the MYO quickly gained members in academic institutions and started to influence the military, government officials, and the peasantry. The organization's ostensible objective was simply to alert the nation to the anti-Islamic perils of Communism. Throughout the country, however, there began to flare rumors that the organization's primary goal was, like the PDPA, to topple Zahir Shah's corrupt government. Unlike the PDPA, however, the MYO would proceed to establish an Islamic form of government and abolish, once and for all, the infections of despotism and Communism.

The primary founders became the executive committee members of the organization. They were Professor Mawlavi Habiburahman, Engineer Habiburahman, Abdulqader Tawana, Khwaja Mahfouz, Saifuddin Nasratyar, Engineer Gulbuddin Hekmatyar, and Habib Hanani.

In the following months, while Khalq and Parcham competed for members among the urban elite, the MYO ideologue won support in the cities and the provinces alike. The nontraditional values of Marxist thought found little acceptance or insignificance in rural communities, and since most Afghan city-dwellers had come from the rural, traditional way of life, the two Marxist factions found that their greatest competition for members was not with each other but with the young Muslim organization.

This fact apparently disturbed someone enough to commit murder, though it is difficult to speculate who may have actually been responsible. The tool was a member of the medical staff at Kabul University, who, upon receiving Abdu Rahim Niazi for routine treatment, administered something other than medicine. When MYO sources discovered their leader had been poisoned, a vast circuit was put to work, and within hours, Niazi was on a flight to India, where competent doctors were waiting to save his life.

Help had come too late. Abdu Rahim Niazi died before his plane reached New Delhi. His funeral was accompanied by a procession of hundreds of thousands of Kabul citizens with the resounding shouts of "Allah-hu-Akbar" ("God is the Greatest").

The plot to weaken the core of the Muslim Youth Organization (which was becoming increasingly known as *Ikhwan-ul-Muslimeen*, or "the Muslim Brotherhood") had effectively backfired.

In the 1971 Kabul University Student Union's election, all political groups participated. Both Engineer Nasratyar and Engineer Gulbuddin Hekmatyar from engineering and the American-sponsored faculty, and Engineer Habiburahman from polytechnic, a Soviet-sponsored faculty, were elected. This gave majority seats to the MYO.

The organization's popularity at the university grew, as did its membership. Most prominent among the new wave of recruits were university lecturers, particularly Ghulam Muhammad Niazi, Prof. Abdul Rasul Sayyaf, and Prof. Burhanuddin Rabbani, a teacher of the Sharia of Islamic law.

Influence and determination continued to strengthen for Marxists and Muslims alike. The coming years promised, if anything, challenge.

The coming of the new decade heralded the final throes of King Zahir's weakening power. The experiment in liberal democracy had deteriorated into a devious struggle for survival by the current government, while criticism of Zahir's tactics mounted on all sides. Foreign trade arrangements lapsed as participating nations grew impatient with Afghanistan's tangled economy. Even the Soviet Union withheld aid. The crisis was aggravated by a severe drought, followed by a famine in which nearly half a million Afghans perished.

The king's neglect became alarmingly clear. His administration had taken the steps necessary to modernize the country but had failed to develop the organization to manage it. Pressure from political groups and civil unrest culminated in riots in several instances. Zahir attempted to appease his public by replacing his prime ministers, one after another. First, he appointed Noor Ahmad Etemadi, then Dr. Mohammed Zahir, and then Mosa Shafiq. Regardless, foreign policy remained unstable, the Parliament increasingly failed to solve internal problems, and corruption continued to spread.

The nation wanted food and provisions, not new prime ministers. Restlessness became turmoil.

In 1973, King Zahir Shah and Queen Humaira retreated to Italy, officially for "medical treatment."

On July 17, in the absence of the king, Mohammed Daoud arrived in Kabul, accompanied by various leftist military officers and Parchamis and a number of army units. In a few hours, Daoud was returned to power; this time, absolute. The nearly bloodless coup had claimed a mere eight lives. The absence of any real defense of Zahir's regime was a mystery. Associated officers later learned that there had been some kind of understanding and arrangement between Daoud and Zahir. The deposed king would never return to Afghanistan. On the evening of July 17, 1973, Daoud's voice was heard throughout the nation on the regular Radio Kabul broadcast. It was announced that the monarchy had been overthrown and that Daoud was founder, president, and prime minister of a new republic.

The kingdom, which had been the single politically unifying force in the tribal land of Afghanistan since the time of Ahmad Shah Baba, no longer existed.

As had been promised, several key figures in the coup—all of them Parchamis—were given prime posts in the new administration. Faiz Muhammad, a senior member of Parcham, was named minister of the interior. Abdul Qader, a former officer of Zahir's military, became deputy commander of the air force. Pacha Gul became minister of the frontier. Mohammed Khan Jalaler became minister of trade and commerce. Additional positions in development, education, and agriculture were imparted to members of the Parcham party.

The official Soviet newspaper, *Pravda*, reported the transfer of power in somewhat exaggerated terms, calling it an "Afghan revolution," denoting, perhaps, a vast consensus of the Afghan people. In truth, the tribal masses had never ceased their opposition to Daoud, and opposition to Parcham ideologies was almost universal, outside cosmopolitan centers.

While the Soviet Union, not surprisingly, became the first to extend recognition to the new regime, mutineer Afghans plotted a counter-coup. Maswat ("Equality"), a tentative organization led by Mohammad Hashim Maiwandwal, a former prime minister under Zahir Shah, staged an attack on Daoud's Kabul stronghold a mere thirty-three days after the coup. Daoud's renegade army quickly thwarted Maiwandwal's hasty action. Days later, Maswat's leader was found dead, killed in execution style.

Daoud spent the ensuing months following the predicted pro-Soviet foreign policy. Resurrecting his beloved Pashtunistan cause, he ardently reversed Afghanistan's recent friendship with Pakistan. But this was remarkably temporary.

During the first two years of the presidency, Parcham exercised a considerable amount of power in Afghanistan's central government. Then, as 1975 approached, Daoud, as if by design, began to dilute the party's effectiveness. He sent Faiz Muhammad as ambassador to Indonesia. Pacha Gul was sent as ambassador to Bulgaria. Other Communist elements were simply dismissed. Radio Kabul announced that Bakhtari, minister of agriculture, and Abdul Hamid Mohtat, also a minister, had been dismissed on the grounds of "failing to fulfill their responsibilities."

Apparently, Daoud had become uncomfortable with his energetic allies, though he could not openly oppose them without provoking their friends in Moscow.

Beyond the bustling streets of Kabul, however, the realities obliged no such diplomacy. Constantly provoked by corrupt Parchamis posted throughout the frontier, the tribal khans frequently revolted in minor incidents that were rarely taken seriously by the administration.

Then, on a day in July 1975, in a place called Panjshir, a fertile valley near the Hindu Kush mountain range north of Kabul, the local villagers earned the attention of Daoud, the Soviet Politburo, and even the world press. Unable to resolve their differences with the local government, the people of the valley united in an armed uprising in which the assigned governor of Panjshir, a Parchami, was killed.

The insurgents controlled the area for nearly two weeks. Control was abruptly returned to Daoud by a strafing air raid by Kabul's air force.

Although the scale of the Panjshir revolt would not be repeated during Daoud's administration, such disturbances were not uncommon. It is unlikely that MYO affiliates were the agitators behind every incident, but this was a popular belief around Kabul, a belief the MYO worked hard to perpetuate. Fearful of the Communist's persistent influence in their country, particularly after the coup, MYO leadership resolved to take military action and was less than humble in their admission of it. Indeed, they could scarcely deny it, as a number of the organization's most reputable members already had been captured in the provinces in the wake of small hit-and-run guerrilla operations. Before the end of Daoud's administration, most of MYO's leadership would be captured and executed by the regime: Eng. Habiburahman, Khwaja Mahfouz, and Dr. Omar, captured in Kabul; Prof. Mawlavi Habiburahman, captured in Laghman; Eng. Nasratyar, captured in Herat—all were killed. Of the founders, only Eng. Hekmatyar survived the trial for some years. Operations in almost a dozen provinces cost the organization hundreds of members to imprisonment or death.

Though the struggles in the countryside brought little immediate political change, the sharp differences between traditional and socialist thought were brought into clearer nationwide focus, and as the struggle between right and left emerged from university hallways and entered international headlines, a sort of fresh, bracing awareness began to arise in the hearts of many divided Afghans—an awareness of a deeper, stronger unifying force than the kingship had ever been. Bureaucrats, farmers, military officers, merchants, and nomads throughout Afghanistan were beginning to feel the unifying force of Islam.

Daoud himself was not immune to the ascending sense of Muslim brotherhood among the faithful. As his confreres at the Kremlin stirred uneasily, Daoud ventured yet a bolder step away from Moscow. Still wary of the scope of Russia's importance to the prosperity of Afghanistan, Shah Reza Pahlavi of Iran again intervened, urging Daoud to meet with Pakistan's recent prime minister, Zulfikar Ali Bhutto. Still working to calm the social shock wave reverberating from the Indian invasion and the violent part of East Pakistan into Bangladesh in 1972, Bhutto was naturally eager to secure friendship with his neighbor to the west, particularly if it meant a more comfortable temperament among the Pathans and Baluch of former West Pakistan. As Bhutto hoped, a number of cooperative agreements resulted from the meeting, including an earnest agreement to bury, once and for all, the issue of Pashtunistan.

The government of the United States, anxious over its interests in South Asia, happily awarded $40 million in aid to Daoud's regime.

Iran's government, also pleased with Daoud's new amiability toward Pakistan, invited Daoud's special envoy, his brother, Muhammad Naeem, to come to Teheran to discuss issues of bilateral interest. Naeem returned to Kabul with the first installment of a ten-year aid agreement that had been arrived at in 1974. The most important item of the agreement was to be the construction of a railroad link along the American-carved road to Iran's Mashhad Province via Islam Qalah. The railroad would provide an efficient and permanent trade route between Kabul and the Western world. Iran's total aid to Afghanistan over the next decade was to equal $2 billion.

Endowments from a number of Arab nations followed. The Organization of Petroleum Exporting Countries (OPEC) was enjoying increasing prosperity and was in the auspicious position in 1976 to establish the OPEC Fund for International Development to technically and economically aid developing countries. Afghanistan was among the fund's first recipients.

The growing generosity of the Muslim world toward its Afghan nation assured a considerable deterioration of Daoud's customary high degree of dependence on the Soviet Union. Already, in fact, the Teheran agreement had made Iran Afghanistan's chief benefactor, emphatically replacing the USSR.

At this time, Gulbuddin Hekmatyar, recently revealed as a guiding leader of military uprisings in major provinces, was enjoying a measure of international acclaim. His burgeoning suborganization, Hezb-i-Islami Afghanistan (Islamic Party of Afghanistan), was the only military division of the MYO with a significant reputation.

Qazi Waqad, another leading member of the MYO—unattached but involved with several MYO divisions—encouraged the coalition of Hekmatyar's organization and Prof. Burhanuddin Rabani's organization, Jamiat-i-Islami Afghanistan (Islamic Society of Afghanistan). The groups successfully united under the accepted leadership of Qazi Waqad and began operating from common headquarters in Peshawar.

Regardless of Daoud's recent congeniality with the Muslim world, internal policies continued to suppress Islamic activism and, at least marginally, were sympathetic toward Communism. Restive Afghans, therefore, would continue armed rebellion, though with relaxed fervor.

The USSR in 1977 sent a somewhat frigid invitation to Daoud, who agreed to visit Moscow and meet with Soviet leader Leonid Brezhnev in April. According to a member of the Afghan delegation, Brezhnev imprudently greeted Daoud with a virtual barrage of accusations and inquiries. Finally, upon being asked to explain an alleged visit by Muhammad Naeem to Washington, DC, Daoud rose irately from his conference chair and said, in effect, "I am the president of an independent and nonaligned country, not one of your East European vassals. No one has the right to ask me such questions."

With indignant resolve, the president returned to Kabul and proceeded to replace and dismiss all suspected Communists in the military and the parliament. The replacements to the cabinet were solely elected by Daoud, so that his "democratic" council became a personal puppet, constructed of friends, relatives, and sycophants. Next, Daoud renovated the constitution, introducing an amendment that would allow only one political party to exercise influence in Afghanistan—his own. The new party, called Meli-Ghorzang, or National Revolutionary Party, was prudently internationalist in its lobbying, with a decided bias toward the nonaligned world. The leftists, without leaving town, were exiled.

So, during what had become a routine conversation at an informal soiree at the Soviet embassy in Kabul, which Taraki, Amin, and Babrak regularly attended, the rather ill-humored leaders of Khalq and Parcham reluctantly submitted to the decade-old unofficial pressure of Alexander Puzanov, Soviet ambassador to Afghanistan, and agreed to reunite. Although the alliance reassumed the original name of PDPA, its members would never quite shed their separate identities as Khalqis and Parchamis, and unity never reached deeper than a temporary sharing of political resources. Taraki was granted his previous position as head chairman of the party, perhaps because Babrak had so radically failed to woo the support of the Afghan populace.

Regardless of any tenuous cooperation, the PDPA continued in 1978 to be without friends at the palace, and Daoud continued his trajectory away from Moscow. Seeking to relay a positive response to Daoud, Prof. Burhanuddin Rabbani opted to relax Islamic resistance. A graduate of the tranquil Al-Azhar University in Egypt, Rabbani firmly believed in the conclusive power of education and decided to seek a cold war. Qazi Waqad and Gulbuddin Hekmatyar felt that disarming now would be premature and voted to wait a while longer. As a result, Waqad's coalition dissolved, and Rabbani and Hekmatyar went their separate ways. It was to be learned much later that Daoud, at that very time, had been in conference with Zulfikar Ali Bhutto in the beautiful garrisoned city of Lahore in Punjab, Pakistan, requesting the mediation of Bhutto's government between the leaders of Islamic resistance in Peshawar and Daoud's government. Daoud was seeking reconciliation with his people.

Within only a few months, early in 1978, Daoud made additional visits to India, Yugoslavia, Turkey, Iran, Kuwait, Saudi Arabia, Egypt, and Libya—all members of the international Non-Aligned Movement (NAM). Upon return to Kabul, Daoud's most surprisingly enthusiastic comments were made about the Pakistanis, whom he referred to as "our Muslim brothers."

Furthermore, increased friendliness was displayed toward the United States and Japan, and a development project was planned with the People's Republic of China, with whom the Soviets had grown quite bitter. Moscow must have trembled.

The precarious temperament of the opposing ideologies had been pushed too far. The reckless journey of one man had ripened in the extreme, and on a crisp morning in April, a chain of events would be ignited that would rapidly escalate beyond the wildest fears of that one man. Ultimately, an entire nation would be plunged into the darkest age of its violent history.

On that fateful morning in April, Ali Ahmad Khuram, Afghanistan's minister of planning, was assassinated in front of his office. Within hours, Daoud's intelligence network discovered that certain Communist elements were behind the assassination, and a number of PDPA members were arrested.

The next assassination took place on April 18. Mir Akbar Khyber, editor in chief of Parcham's periodical, was shot to death.

Reliable sources close to Hafizullah Amin at the time told me that Amin himself had contracted the killing of Khyber, who apparently had printed material that Amin found disagreeable.

The PDPA, naturally, accused the regime of killing a Parchami in retaliation for the death of Ali Ahmad Khuram, and a massive demonstration was organized to accompany Khyber's funeral procession. Five thousand demonstrators marched through the streets of the capital, shouting anti-American, anti-CIA (America's secret service), and anti-regime slogans. The frightening display of might ended in clashes with the police.

Understandably shaken, Daoud hastily decided that his next move should be to try to isolate the zealous leaders of PDPA. On April 26, Radio Kabul announced on its regular 8:00 p.m. broadcast that the conspiring agents of foreigners, Taraki and Babrak, had been arrested.

It seems, however, that the arrest of these individuals was not enougouh to inhibit the anti-governmental activities of the PDPA leadership. While the cabinet discussed the fate of the Communists, Amin, from his home, was able to send to Aslam Watanjar and Abdul Qader, officers who had helped place Daoud in power, instructions on how to overthrow him.

Twelve hours after Radio Kabul's broadcast—at 8:00 a.m. on April 27—fifty-seven tanks surrounded the presidential palace, under the command of Colonel Muhammed Omar, a Parchami, and Colonel Aslam Watanjar, a Khalqi.

The author was a student at Kabul University, located less than two miles west of the palace, and easily heard the sounds of machine-gun fire, artillery explosions, and heavy bombardment. Breathless curiosity drew me and many others to the source of the unexplained and frightful disturbance. It was an outrageous scene—cars honking, people yelling, gun blasts, flying rubble, and the lifeless bodies of civilians sprawled in the streets.

Daoud's sizeable Republican Guard proved a challenging resistance. Colonel Omar was finished, along with his tank, by a hand grenade thrown by a guard. As the firefight zone spread to other parts of the city, a number of tanks continued to shell the palace, causing heavy casualties.

Meanwhile, most divisions lingered on the outskirts of Kabul, quite undecided about which side to fight for. Major General Ghulam Haider Rasuli, Daoud's loyal defense minister, decided to risk a mad dash through the city to make a personal request for assistance to the prominent Reshkhor Division. In a daring escape, the major general maneuvered an automobile out of the palace, through the barrage, and into the chaos of Kabul. Ironically, his vehicle was incapacitated suddenly by a traffic accident. Badly injured, he continued toward the outskirts on foot but was spotted by PDPA forces and gunned down.

Early in the afternoon, Soviet MiG fighter aircraft appeared overhead, firing rockets and dropping bombs on the palace in two consecutive attacks. Soon after, I spoke to an officer of the Reshkhor Division, who told me that the body of a Soviet pilot had been retrieved from a MiG-21 shot down east of the city. Later, it was learned that thousands of Soviet advisors, invited by their friend Daoud, had accompanied PDPA units.

A third attack by a MiG-21, piloted by Col. Abdul Qader, effectively crushed the Republican Guard, and by 2:00 p.m., the drama was over. Much of the palace was destroyed.

According to a former officer who would later defect to the Islamic resistance, Daoud and his brother, Muhammad Naeem, were captured alive. Daoud's wife, children (including his daughter, Zarlakhta, a literature student in my class at Kabul University), and grandchildren were all killed during the fighting. Daoud and Naeem were never seen again.

At 7:00 p.m., the voice of Col. Qader was broadcast throughout Afghanistan. He announced, simply, that Daoud had been eliminated and that the age of the mohammadzai (the royal family) had finally come to an end.

This unsettling announcement bred anxious speculation throughout the provinces. Who had deposed the president? Who would succeed him? Many hoped the MYO was behind the coup. Many feared otherwise.

On its regular 8:00 p.m. broadcast, on the last day of April 1978, Radio Kabul announced that Noor Muhammad Taraki was president, prime minister, and chairman of the Revolutionary Council of a new regime. Babrak Karmal was vice president and deputy prime minister. Hafizullah Amin was deputy prime minister and minister of foreign affairs. Communism had settled like a stone.

This was the culmination of the twentieth century, and the Caesars of the third Rome, called Moscow, stood on the threshold of their ultimate aspirations in the south. The warmth of the Arabian Sea and the riches of oil from the Persian Gulf beckoned. For a moment, stillness pervaded the air in the land of the Afghans.

4

In the Spirit of
Genghis Khan

It was called the "Saur" (or, April) Revolution, an appropriate
name for a of the Great October Revolution. In the weeks following
the takeover, Taraki insisted to the nervous Western world that the new
regime was associated with non-alignedmovement non-Communist,
sending the trusting but confused embassies of capitalism in Kabul
scrambling to assemble their dossiers on Taraki, Amin, and Babrak.
Foreign aid from all donors would continue, at least until the West could
evaluate Taraki's claims and ascertain whether he would or would not
align with the Soviet Union.

For the PDPA's rivals of thirteen years, throughout Afghanistan,
and in exile, there could be no question of Taraki's intentions. Auxiliaries
of Islamic resistance crowded around frontier radios and television
sets to hear the familiar rhetoric of masked Communism, the PDPA's
traditional instrument of wooing support for their otherwise unpopular
cause. An early contrivance frequently used by both Taraki and Amin was
a speech about the regime's "respect for Islam," an absurd proposition
in view of past policies of the Central Committee. The broadcasts were
of small consequence. Even in the remotest of villages, where a person's
only notions of the outside world were the words from a radio, the new
government seemed alien at best. "Respect for Islam," clearly the evasive
words of *kafirs* (infidels), was usually followed by a speech hinting at some

untraditional reforms that potentially could touch even the remotest of Afghans.

For a devout Muslim, it is unacceptable to be ruled by infidels, but nonetheless, most Afghans were willing to give the new government a chance. After all, before protest, one at least should wait for the rulers to do something "ungodly."

Toward this end, the regime, pushed on by an impatient Amin, did not hesitate. Amin seemed to feel that slow reform was inefficient, and if the peasants couldn't keep pace, that was their calamity—they would have to find a quiet way to adjust.

Amin's impatience was not reserved for the peasants. The coup had been an unchallenged success. The cooperation of Khalq and Parcham, under the encouragement and supervision of Moscow, undeniably had placed victory in the hands of the revolutionaries. Afghanistan now belonged to the Communists. Gratified, the Soviet Union was first to extend diplomatic recognition, followed in swift course by many other nations.

Almost immediately, Moscow rewarded her Afghan comrades with increased military aid, including advisors, until fifteen thousand Soviet technicians were residing in Afghanistan. But the coup was over, and cooperation expired, and the three top men of the Revolutionary Council resumed their dual rivalry.

Amin and Babrak were particularly bitter. Babrak continued his crafty loyalty hunts in the military, and Amin found it increasingly unbearable to share power with his Parchami foe.

Amin's salvation seemed to come when the ASGA (Afghan Secret Service) uncovered a conspiracy in the Parcham camp. It was revealed to Taraki that Babrak, with a number of Parchami cabinet members, were plotting to oust all members of Khalq from the government, including Taraki and Amin, who were believed to be targeted for assassination. Babrak solicited Abdul Qader, now a major general and minister of defense, but he refused to collaborate with Babrak, probably because of loyalty to Taraki, though Qader was known to dislike Amin.

Taraki and Amin naturally were eager to eliminate their enemies, if only by imprisonment. Nonetheless, probably to their surprise, the Soviets intervened and asked that Babrak and his men be neutralized some other way.

Taraki probably assumed that Moscow was only trying to protect the rather sensitive image of the Afghan Communists. In retrospect, however, it is more likely that Moscow was dissatisfied with Taraki's performance, which had incurred opposition throughout the country, and the Soviets were trying to preserve an alternative leader in Babrak.

Whatever the case, Taraki submitted and sent Babrak as ambassador to Czechoslovakia, Anahita Ratebzad as ambassador to Yugoslavia, Noor Ahmad Noor as ambassador to Great Britain, Mahmud Baryalai as ambassador to Pakistan, and Dr. Najibullah as ambassador to Iran.

It was not enough for Amin, whose impatience apparently overtook him. Within a few weeks, General Qader and various remaining Parchami officials were arrested and charged with treason. Confessions were extracted from Qader, as well as Sultan Ali Kishtmand and Muhammad Rafi, both cabinet members. The confessions and details of the conspiracy were announced on Radio Kabul, as well as printed boldly on the front page of *Hewad* ("Homeland"), the government-run newspaper.

The damage to the sensitive image had been done, and Taraki assumed that Moscow wouldn't mind if he now relieved the Parchami ambassadors of their posts and ordered them home to face the courts. None, however, returned.

The next Radio Kabul announcement accused the Parchamis of embezzling money from the Afghan embassies as follows: $7,500 in Prague; $7,600 in Belgrade; $210,00 in Washington; $2,000 in London; $4,500 in Islamabad (Pakistan's modern capital); and more than $280,000 in Teheran. The money reportedly was used to stay abroad and plot against Taraki. No defense could be devised, as Babrak and the others effectively disappeared, having been secretly adopted by the Soviet Bloc, where they could wait to topple the government.

For now, at least, the regime would have to deal with the more immediate problems of domestic affairs. Amin's "backward peasants" were not quietly adjusting. Overly anxious young men, scarcely out of their universities and completely without experience, were driven to the provincial capitals or unloaded by helicopters in the frontier and left to govern a people about whom they were completely ignorant and in whom they had no interest. Thousands of years of traditional tribal rule by local elders and powerful khans was expected to be relinquished, so that youngsters from an alien place could set about demolishing the ancient way of life of these curious Afghans. The immediate uprisings in several quarters of Afghanistan overwhelmed the young Communist governors there. Those who survived fled back to Kabul, closely followed by anyone who had been loyal to them.

Indeed, several provinces had become Islamic republics unto themselves, completely disconnected with Kabul. In the provincial capitals, the Communist governors, with their assigned military units, were able to maintain arbitrary control, but only during daylight hours. At night, the resistance took the cities back and wielded command until dawn. Even in Kabul, the curfew hours, 11:00 p.m. to 4:00 a.m., belonged to the resistance. Those urbanites who weren't Communist but who were not ready to take to the night supplied ammunition to the saboteurs, fed them, and harbored them in the daytime.

In many cities and rural villages, the Communists had no footing at all, and the original inhabitants were able to reopen schools, regenerate commerce, and put public transportation back in service. Tribal political and judicial systems resumed.

Meanwhile, Kabul was flooded by waves of reformers fleeing the frontier and seeking refuge where at least a semblance of security existed. Many reformers became reacquainted with the families from which they had been snatched in early childhood, to be sent to school by a man named Daoud. As kinship is such an integral part of Afghan life, these young Communists, fleeing to the capital by the hundreds, brought family members with them by the tens of thousands. By November 1978, Kabul was overburdened by its population, and with the nation's economy dismembered, inflation was rapid. The monthly rent of an apartment had been 350 afs ($50 US), but it was now 2,000 Afs ($300). A slab of naan (flatbread) had been three afs but now it was an ordeal to find it for any less than none afs.

The Taraki administration wasn't suffering. As Marxists, their prescribed ideal was a classless society, but in these times of tribulation, when the governed went hungry, the Communist officials grew fat in the company of servants in the luxurious homes and offices they had confiscated after the revolution. As the citizens of Kabul and other cities waited solemnly in the barren tea houses, local officials sped through the streets in post cars to prove whose was the fastest and the best,

Taraki's reforms persisted, enforced by Amin's methods, without consideration of traditions. Those who resisted or who were even suspected of opposing the central government were taken from their villages, imprisoned, and often executed. Even members of the party sometimes disappeared. Innocent women and children were incarcerated to punish male family members suspected of being involved with the resistance. In the prisons, brutal torturing ensued, including such psychological torture as sleep deprivation and reprogramming. There are accounts by prisoners who escaped and joined the resistance of elderly couples being buried alive by prison guards who considered them useless and too weak to survive much longer anyway.

Those who were allowed to remain in their communities were forced to submit to ruthless change. Homes were forcibly occupied for meetings of the Sazman-i-Jawanan (the Afghan Young Communist League) and other party activities to direct the reforms.

Arranged marriages were outlawed and dowries and compensations were forbidden, so that sanctioned alliances between clans were no longer possible, and a girl's marriage became an irredeemable economic loss to her family.

Land reform was perhaps the greatest blow to the traditional social structure. The first plank of the Communist manifesto calls for the abolition of all private property. Amanullah Khan abandoned the idea in the 1920s, but his army was not nearly as powerful or capable as Taraki's. In 1978, threats of imprisonment and the overwhelming ability to carry out those threats were sufficient to set in motion the exchange of land-ownership deeds in motion.

The Soviets used land reform in the bloody wake of the Bolshevik Revolution to ensure that the masses wouldn't be able to feed themselves and would be forced to adopt the policies of Marxist socialism. The state would provide everything for everyone. The Communist propaganda line was that land reform was to prevent the "atrocious amassing of wealth or monopolizing of property." The Afghan disciples of Marxism, eager to duplicate the Soviet socialist scheme, probably endeavored to equate the tribal chieftains of the Afghan frontier with the deposed czars of Russia, a clumsy comparison at best.

In traditional Afghanistan, local khans ruled over small regions, sometimes encompassing several villages, sometimes a single estate, and sometimes a mobile convoy of nomads. The khan owned the land of the animals, and when challenged, would fight to the death, although not often his own. His people received protection from intruders as well as the shared benefits of the crops of the caravan. In this way, society endured in an otherwise lawless land for countless centuries.

Land reform disrupted all of this. The intruding Communists divided the land into standardized plots that were distributed among the farmers, with no compensation for the original land owner. The farmers, who had been working the land all along and reaping its benefits, could not afford the seeds, fertilizer, animals and equipment needed for agriculture, all of which had been the charge of the khan. Feudal trade institutions had been outlawed, so there was no way for the farmer to gain his own supplies.

Most distressing of all to the land recipient was the injury to his religious beliefs. The Quran forbids the Muslim to steal or accept stolen property, but faced with execution, many farmers assented, if only temporarily. Others, foreseeing no future retribution, took their own lives, as it was more honorable to go to paradise by one's own hand than to disobey the laws of Allah Almighty.

Taraki undoubtedly believed he was improving the lives of his people, but he failed to show any respect for the people's own desires for their lives. Perhaps in Russia the peasants were grateful to receive plots of land, but Afghanistan is not like Russia. Some well-informed sources in Kabul reported to intelligence in Peshawar that resistance fighters, captured by Afghan (and later by Soviet) troops often had government deeds of land ownership in their pockets.

Invasion of time-honored tribal autonomy, ridicule of deeply rooted customs, and casual disregard for Islamic law may have been enough to spawn a massive rebellion, eventually. Nevertheless, the final intrusion of the mosque, which maddened ever the sanest, most peaceful man, was the defilement of the most sacred place in the Afghan's life. These are the far pavilions of the Near East, whether a humble mud-brick cubicle or a beautiful structure of arches, fountains, and tile. This is where the faithful come to stand, side by side, facing Mecca, and bow before their God.

The Communists came to preach atheism, and they took the mosque as their pulpit. Religious leaders were ordered to abandon the Quran and read instead from Marx's *Manifesto* and works by Lenin. The people of the villages or cities were ordered to listen, but when tearful *mullahs (priests)* used Taraki's name in the Friday prayer (as armed guards and officials stood nearby, the congregations walked out).

The regime's profanity won it a full-scale armed rebellion. It was declared a struggle for the freedom of the land, a jihad, by Islamic leaders. What began in the wilds of the Pamir and the Hindu Kush grew so artlessly that the messengers of jihad ran with the rivers into the valleys and lowlands. They were a different kind of fighter; they waged a war in the way of Allah they were freedom fighters. The Communists would now face these fighters—the mujahideen.

The first signal to the PDPA back in Kabul that their original enemies had returned from exile in Peshawar was a rather frantic message from a military unit stationed in the valley of Shegal, in the mountainous Konar Province. It seemed their position in the village of Karhala was under attack in a barrage of rifle fire from the surrounding mountainsides.

A group of mujahideen with worn-out British Enfield rifles had settled on the rocky slopes and fired on the military post with what they had, many of these rifles were over a century old and veterans of the British-Afghan wars. The soldiers fired back with Kalashnikovs—Soviet-made assault rifles with both semi-automatic and automatic fire capabilities, more familiar in the West as the AK-47 (Automatic Kalashnikov 1947).

The battle raged awkwardly, but with fervor, for two days and nights. The mujahideen were winning. According to Commander Kashmir, a mujahid, the military unit commander contacted him by wireless radio and offered to surrender his men. Kashmir immediately agreed to a cease-fire. It seemed the mujahideens' first campaign had been a success.

Two hours passed uneasily as the mujahideen held council, and the military unit waited quietly.

Then, a low rumble of aircraft engines was heard from the south, and a Soviet personnel carrier appeared in the still air, high above the valley. Within minutes, a second plane appeared, and then a third. The formidable hulks moved lethargically over Karhala, dropping trails of tumbling objects that fell toward the earth for a few seconds and then paused, suddenly, beneath blossoming, gray parachutes. The mujahideen watched in dread as reinforcement troops filled the sky. Refreshed rage exploded from the Karhala outpost.

Heavy casualties were inflicted on both sides. The mujahideen lost sixty-three men and finally withdrew from Shegal, dispersing to unknown places.

Soviet advisors in Karhala believed that the outskirts of the village had sheltered wounded fighters and that many villagers had fed the insurgents and even fought alongside them.

An Afghan soldier, who later deserted, gives an account of what followed:

"Using soldier's whips, they summoned the people to the village's largest mosque to listen to the provincial governor. Shocked by the treason of their own nationals, [the people] gathered in front of the tyrant, who ordered the men to proceed to the provincial administration building, fifty meters away. There, the men were lined up and searched, and whatever they had was taken away. A Russian comrade ordered the soldiers to open fire, and in just a few moments, the men were cut to the ground as their women and children watched. The village lost all its menfolk to the unchecked, malicious, revenge of these tyrants. Every male over fourteen years old was killed. The victims numbered 1,166 innocent human beings. Some of the men who were not killed instantaneously by the bullets threw themselves into the river in a desperate move to flee. A young child, terrorized by the scene of the massacre, fell dead. Karhala became bode of widows, orphans . . ."

The so-called "Red Battle" of the resistance spread rapidly to every domain of the Afghans, even beyond the borders. Hundreds of thousands of oppressed Muslims joined the revolt, many roused by the organization's leaders who moved between bases in Afghanistan, Pakistan, and Iran; most joined of their own initiative. Even isolated groups, like the Shiite Hazaras of Hazarajat in central Afghanistan, revolted.

The simple, primary tactic used against a superior army with superior weapons was devised by the Afghans in their wars against the British: in the absence of a solid enemy front (which the topography of Afghanistan made impossible), attack the enemy's stronghold, or convoy from above and then retreat and dissolve into the impenetrable mountains before the enemy can retaliate.

The Communist military eventually would learn that it could combat the tactic effectively only by being higher than the attackers. Ruthless attacks by gunship helicopters and MiG fighter jets would become the primary tactic of the regime. Meanwhile, offensive aircraft would serve in retaliation. In the absence of the "rebels" and with little hope of finding any, innocent citizens were killed. Entire villages were bombed and strafed. Any panic-stricken villagers seen fleeing into the countryside were pursued by helicopters and machine-gunned.

In the cities, ten-year-old boys who belonged to the Sazman Jawanan were armed with Kalashnikovs and ordered to "kill the reactionaries and agents of Imperialism." These children, hardly comprehending the finality of death, blasted the heads off anyone they chose—rebels, Communists, party members, family members, and disagreeable playmates.

Every party member was authorized to "execute counter-revolutionaries at any time." Within six months, almost every family or clan would lose a member. Within a year, almost half a million refugees would quail to camps outside the borders of their homeland in Pakistan and Iran, and the ragged progression of homeless would continue to drain Afghanistan of population for years. It is conceivable that the Soviets, advising Taraki's military, had intended this effect, perhaps hoping that the Pashtunistan they had worked so hard to propagate would become a reality and all the devout of Afghanistan could live there and weaken Pakistan, who at that time ardently condemned the Communist regime in Kabul.

In fact, the flow of refugees disadvantaged the regime. Aside from the grim world opinion that any refugee population tends to generate, the Taraki regime now faced the scrutiny of the United Nations, whose confreres readily interviewed the excommunicated of Afghanistan. The criminal nature of the regime was slowly and cautiously revealed to the world's nations.

The flow of refugees also served to reunite hundreds and later thousands of diverted members of the MYO, who joined the factions of their beloved organization and returned to Afghanistan as mujahideen, armed and organized.

As 1978 ended, Gulbuddin Hekmatyar's organization, Hezb-i-Islami, sent a detachment of mujahideen to Konar Province, from which had come news of an impending uprising against the murderous governor there.

It was a brief battle. The administrators in Kabul would soon learn that Konar was in the hands of the "rebels" and that the 9th Mountain Brigade of Asmar had deserted and joined the mujahideen.

The provincial governor—the "tyrant" of Karhala, who had achieved notoriety as Nizamuddin the Ungodly—was shot by his personal bodyguard. The body was dragged into the street and hacked to pieces. For the next eight months, Konar was governed by its people.

The deserting Asmar Brigade brought with them thousands of Kalashnikovs, mortars, and ammunition, thirty-five tanks and armored vehicles, and two MI-24, or Hind, gunship helicopters. It was an astounding gain for the mujahideen.

Similar successes were reported from other provinces. In Baghlan, Badakhshan, Ghour, Nangarhar, Paktia, Kandahar, and Bamian rebel forces attacked military convoys and strongholds—and won. Hundreds of Afghan soldiers refused to fight their Muslim brothers and deserted, bringing with them cannons, anti-aircraft weapons, RPG rocket launchers, and anything else they had.

Even the semblance of security in Kabul was rapidly eroding. On February 22, as intrepid demonstrators in Cota-i-Sangi District peacefully protested recent party activities, a police unit arrived and opened fire, killing eighty-six people. Only moments later, in Chandawal District, a mile from the palace, a mob of urbanized Hazaras stormed and looted the police station, seizing the store of machine guns and turning them on the staggered police. Twelve officers were killed, including a woman officer (a phenomenon of the socialist system).

On March 11, just north of Kabul and near Paghman, Kabul's neighboring city; a unit of 120 infantrymen of Qargha Division deserted and joined the mujahideen.

Days later, farther north, rebels armed with Kalashnikovs and RPG rocket launchers attacked Bagram Air Base and destroyed an armored personnel carrier and two MiG-17 subsonic interceptors, whose deafening explosions shattered windows on the base and sent flames that were seen by the citizens of Kabul forty miles away.

In the far west of Afghanistan, the Dari-speaking Persian tribes of the Tajik and the Kazilbash joined the insurgence with a feat that impressed Kabul and Moscow alike. The massive revolt began in the city of Herat on March 19, and within hours, an entire military division stationed in the province turned on their superiors and merged with the rebels in an awesome battle against the provincial Communist forces. An enormous amount of artillery fell to the citizens, and every man, woman, and child who could hold a weapon supported the rebellion.

A great number of Khalqis and Parchamis were killed, perhaps over a thousand. Those who survived the fighting were stoned to death in the streets. The seventy-one Soviet and Czech advisors who were killed were decapitated, their heads stuck on lances and the lances stuck in the earth.

The deserting soldiers who had, under orders, persecuted Herat, were welcomed by women throwing *Qand* (Afghan candy) from the rooftops as the men marched by.

The conquest of Herat Province, several times larger and more populous than that of Konar, placed the most strategic region of the west in the domain of the resistance.

Kabul was in turmoil. Amin was anguished and frustrated and demanded that his rank be elevated to prime minister and deputy of the Revolutionary Council. Taraki refused.

Opposing loyalties had developed in the military and now, the Khalqis were divided. Amin, in his competition with Babrak, had won the patronage of many influential officers, and Taraki found himself helpless to stop the discharge and replacement of nearly all his allies in the military. Since there was no irrefutable evidence that Amin had ordered the replacements, and any divided loyalties were improvable, no official accusations of treachery could be brought against Amin. Taraki had to remain silent in a thickening atmosphere of utter mistrust.

Nor would charges be brought against Amin's military friends, who acted without consent of their commander in chief. After the upheaval in Herat, Taraki hardly wished to antagonize the divisions in Kabul. Instead, cooperation in smashing the resistance continued.

A mere two weeks after the Herat revolt, airborne troops at Shindand, the Soviet-built air base fifty miles from Herat, were ordered to lay siege to the defiant province. Understanding that the nature of the mission would not merely "eliminate the agents of Imperialism" but pitilessly destroy thousands of fellow Afghans as well, the pilots refused to participate.

The administration accepted this; a phone call was made to Moscow, and a formation of Soviet-piloted MiG-19s thundered across the Afghan-Soviet border on approach to Herat.

The city and almost all the villages were bombed and strafed in brutal and relentless consecutive attacks. A raging storm of explosions and blasts of rubble and searing heat rocked the terrified region for hour after merciless hour.

The villagers who had heard the horrible barrage coming and were able to escape to hide in caves in the wilderness would return to find level earth where their villages had been and a moonscape of stones and craters where their fields had been, their annual crops and food supplies decimated.

When finally a hesitant boom resounded across the smoky sky and the savage demons of the air had vanished, the entire province lay in ruin. An eerie, muffled wailing—the haunting symphony of the dying and the mourning—hovered over the region.

The beautiful city of Herat, so long ago reduced to rubble and ash by an army from Mongolia, was once again a silent cemetery of charred and fallen giants. Twenty thousand people were dead. The spirit of Genghis Khan wandered the streets that day . . .

Many educated Marxists in Afghanistan thought it incredible that the Soviets, so passionate in their memorializing the brutal Nazi siege of Leningrad, could enter a neighboring country and so dispassionately repeat the terror. Disillusionment, particularly in the military, was spreading.

Four months passed in the shadow of the Herat tragedy. Neither the military nor the mujahideen could soothe the lingering shock. Morale was low.

Regardless of Taraki's cautious deliberation, antagonism festered around Kabul as a remorseless and increasingly demanding Amin generated hostility as if he intended it. Fellow Khalqis and disheartened patrons in the military grew restless. The regime was losing control and facing a potential counter-revolution in its own camp.

Moscow was rudely alerted to the true digression of its protégé when the twelve hundred soldiers and officers stationed in the Bala-Hissar barracks in central Kabul attempted a mutiny to overthrow the central government, which ultimately could reverse the Communist revolution. The event began unexpectedly on August 6, when an incredible assault of gun and rocket-fire from the Bala-Hissar fort fell upon the tattered and indefensible presidential palace. The weary Communist guard at the palace was hopelessly overwhelmed by the surprise attack, and disoriented ground troops nearby were insufficient relief.

An hour of weakening palace guards and proportionate dread in the administration had passed before Soviet advisors finally roused loyal helicopter pilots into flight.

The swift and bulky Hind gunships dove across the heated sky above the palace, came in low, and rocketed and bombed the barracks, quickly sweeping out of range as heavy explosions tore deep into the buildings. This continued in a series of frantic maneuvers that wreaked erratic destruction across the district.

When the barrage from the burning Bala-Hissar finally ceased and the Hinds glided away, nearly all the twelve hundred mutineers were dead, as were dozens of innocent civilians whose homes had been indiscriminately blasted from the air.

Moscow lost patience. Too much was near to loss.

Taraki was asked to come to Moscow on his way back from a Nonaligned Movement conference in Havana, Cuba. Upon arrival, he was taxied to Red Square and to the familiar Kremlin building, where he was greeted warmly by the bearish Soviet leader, Leonid Brezhnev.

Babrak Karmal attended the meeting, which only mildly surprised Taraki. Informed sources later reported that Taraki's delegation was excluded, but the intent of the meeting was no secret: Brezhnev wanted Amin ousted.

Taraki returned to Kabul on September 11 and, immediately contacted Alexander Pusanov, the Soviet ambassador.

Foreign minister Shah Wali, a member of the delegation, contacted Amin, to whom he was loyal.

On September 14, Taraki heard the Radio Kabul announcement of the dismissal of three powerful cabinet members: Colonel Mohammad Aslam Watanjar, Major Sher Jan Mazdooryar, and Colonel Sayed Muhammad Gulabzoi, all of whom had been outwardly friendly to Taraki and had candidly accused Amin of plotting to oust Taraki. Amin had replaced the men with his own. Taraki's position was weakening, and he would have to act quickly.

When Amin was invited to the palace by his old friend Alexander Puzanov, who insisted that there was no danger and that a simple meeting with Taraki was in order, Amin agreed to come but only in the company of his fifteen-man bodyguard.

As Amin's gang entered the palace, Taraki and his men began shooting, and Amin's men drew their guns and returned fire fervently. The shootout lasted only a few minutes. All of Amin's men were killed or maimed, but Amin was uninjured. He had been saved by Sayed Daoud Taroon, Taraki's personal bodyguard, who was loyal to Amin and had stepped in front of him as he came through the palace doors, sparing him the fatal assault. Sprawled on the dusty, bloody floor, Taraki lay mortally wounded.

Three days later, Radio Kabul's evening broadcast announced that Taraki had graciously resigned his positions for reasons of "poor health." Hafizullah Amin assumed the posts of president, secretary general of the People's Democratic Party, and chairman of the Revolutionary Council. When, during a foreign press conference on September 29, Amin stated that "power is not given but taken," suspicions began to arise about Taraki's illness. (Much later, one of Amin's stooges, an attendant at Jamhuri Hospital, where Taraki was taken, would confess that he had smothered the bedridden president with a toxin-drenched towel.)

Finally, on October 9, Taraki's demise was announced. It was reported that he was buried in his father's burial ground in the small village of Soor Kala, Ghazni Province, where Taraki was born in 1919, eight days before the Bolshevik Revolution. The reported burial has since been refuted, and the true site of the grave is today a mystery.

Taraki was dead, and the people of Afghanistan rejoiced and gave alms. It appeared that Allah had chosen to deliver the oppressed from the hands of evil rulers. Surely the deaths of the other Communists would follow.

Amin's immediate position was quite good. Babrak and now Taraki had been eliminated, and Amin alone would dictate the future of Afghanistan, if he could manipulate support. A series of broadcasts by Amin placed the responsibility for the crimes of the past eighteen months on Taraki, and with Taraki's demise, Amin claimed that security, justice, and democracy would be restored to the nation.

Amin's son, Abdul Rahman, was appointed head of the Afghan Young Communist League. His nephew, Asadullah Amin, became chief of the AGSA (Amin's secrete police). His brother, Abdullah Amin, was sent as governor general to the northern provinces, where he was to tame this most lawless quarter and where he would prove to be as bloodthirsty as his president.

Overshadowing all this gray glory was Amin's unshakable awareness of the Soviets' disappointment. Moscow undoubtedly feared that Amin would carry Afghanistan away from them, as Anwar Sadat had carried away Egypt. And regardless of Amin's tireless efforts to convince Moscow that he would be more loyal than Taraki had been—and indeed, Amin frequently called the Soviet Union "big brother"—Amin had killed their puppet, and there would be a price.

Throughout his own nation, Amin's anticipated popularity refused to take root. His fellow Khalqis, including many who had supported the removal of Taraki, distributed underground *shab-namas* (night letters) condemning the policies of Amin, who was abusing the party for personal profit and arranging the assassinations or executions of any party members who were thought to dislike or disagree with Amin.

Across the frontier, rejoicing fell to lamentation as officers butchered thousands weekly, under the orders of their new commander in chief. The death of Taraki had fertilized an even bloodthirstier regime.

Yet the prosecution of Taraki's memory continued, as if Amin believed that word of his own massacres had not been carried to every part of Afghanistan.

On October 17, the Ministry of the Interior announced that the names of eighteen thousand Afghans who had been executed by Taraki's regime would be posted on the facade of the ministry building.

People came from every province to search for the names of their fathers, mothers, children, and sweethearts. Hundreds crowded in front of the looming building, tearful and breathless, dark with fear and sleeping fury. I was among them. My youngest brother, Hafiz-u-Rahman, had been taken.

A young man near me asked an old, white-bearded man, "*Padar* (father), what has happened to our people? Why are so many killed without having committing crimes?" The elder stared at the ground and slowly shook his head. Another man, standing behind the two, said simply, "Communists rule Afghanistan."

The silence soon parted as names were found and crying and screaming overtook the people. A very young woman in a dark veil found the name of her lost husband, a gallant young military officer who had been taken in 1978. She shouted, "Death to Taraki and Amin! Amin is the Russians' dog!"

A policeman forced his way through the crowd and ordered her to be silent, but she defied him and challenged him to wear the veil, the robe of her grief. He became cowardly and refused. Furious, she challenged any of the policemen to kill her if they dared. One of the policemen stepped forward and shot her through the head.

The crowd exploded, and when the clash was over, sixty-five citizens were dead, most of them elderly men who had lost their families.

The street in front of the ministry building was stained red.

The bitter "Day of 18,000 Martyrs," as it was called, became associated not so much with Taraki's tyranny, as was intended, but with Amin's, which was appropriate, as Amin had been at least equally responsible for the eighteen thousand deaths, and he was still alive. The killing of the mourners had been a spontaneous act of the police, of course, but any sin of the regime naturally clung to the polluted name of Amin.

In the towns of Mazar-i-Sharif and Kandahar and in the provinces of Baghlan, Nangarhar, and Kabul, internal clashes exhausted the demoralized Afghan army, whose troops were losing faith in the distinction between friend and enemy and were turning on each other. At the end of October, a major offensive against the mujahideen in Paktia Province became a disaster for the administration, when the entire Zabul Brigade joined the freedom fighters in crushing the military forces there. Thousands of weapons fell to the rebels, including a number of armored vehicles and tanks.

By November, nearly 70 percent of the army either had deserted or had been killed, so that 85 percent of the country was in mujahideen hands, and the remainder was under enduring siege. In fact, twenty-five thousand fighters had infiltrated Kabul and were armed and ready to overthrow the blight of Afghanistan. But Amin's forces were well-armed and intrepid with the daylight. Guerrilla tactics would range from night to night until, *Insha-Allah* (with God's help), a mujahid might enter the palace.

The black fate of Amin brewed on the horizon.

In the first week of December 1979, Washington, DC, warned of disproportionate military activity in Central Asia and of Soviet forces amassing along the Afghan border. *Pravda*, the Soviet newspaper, called it a "fabrication." US State Department officials insisted that the Soviet

Union was mobilizing its troops, threatening an incredible invasion. It was, of course, true.

The mujahideen, in headquarters outside the country, prayed for their brothers and all the Afghans inside.

It seemed that the true fate of Afghanistan lay not with the Muslims but in the saga of conquest as old as the name of Cyrus the Great, or perhaps in the saga a thousand years older, when Afghanistan was called Bactria and was a geographical obstacle to be overcome.

In any case, Amin had chosen his path, and he would take an entire nation with him.

The land of Afghans would, once again, be plundered.

5

The Bear and the Lion

During the years of internal strife, Afghanistan's geo-political cradle had spiraled into depths of isolation. Pakistan, furious over the United States' inaction when India invaded former East Pakistan, had abandoned friendship with Washington, DC. Subsequent upheavals in Pakistan had plunged the nation into a chaotic period of martial law, culminating with the execution of Zulfikar Ali Bhutto. The chief of staff of the army, General Muhammad Zia-ul-Haq, had assumed power. In Iran, the Islamic Movement had instrumented the fall of the moderate Shah Reza Pahlavi, whose exalted adversary, the proclaimed *ayatollah* ("sign from Allah"), Ruhollah Khomeini, had returned from exile in France to ascend the throne.

The United States, whose post-World II strength in Southwest Asia had endured through Pahlavi and Bhutto, now faced a drastic hostage crisis in Iran and at least uncertainty in Pakistan. Since India actually was aligned with the USSR, all balance against Soviet power in the region at the end of 1979 collapsed.

Recent developments in Soviet-Afghan relations should have charged Kabul's security perception with dread. Yet even when Washington, DC, reported the deployment of massive Soviet armed forces to the Afghan border, Hafizullah Amin continued to behave as if he expected nothing to happen. Soviet advisors effortlessly persuaded him to move his administration to Darul Aman, the aging estate on the outskirts of Kabul that had long been used as the summer palace by former king

Amanullah Khan. Despite the Democratic Guard's unfamiliarity with the logistics of defending the estate, the move was allegedly for "security reasons."

On December 17, AGSA director Asadullah Amin was shot and wounded in a skirmish with the rebels. Visiting Soviet Lieutenant General Viktor Semenovich Paputin, the first deputy minister of internal affairs for the Soviet Union, immediately arranged to have Asadullah flown to Moscow for treatment.

In successive days, other high Afghan officials were neutralized by various policy decisions, and military officers were placed under restrictions. Weapons and equipment of entire divisions were recalled, supposedly for repair and replacement. Every Afghan soldier, except those few who were busily engaged with the nightly rebel attacks, was ordered to "temporarily" disarm. All this seemed to be the sole mandate of the Soviet advisors.

Despite the prevalent disruptions, sabotage, and conflicts, the capital became strangely reticent, as a vague confusion pervaded both the Afghan military and the mujahideen. The Soviets in Kabul, in an almost imperceptible way, suddenly disembarked from the framework of Amin's jurisdiction and began a frenzy of independent activities. Although the reasons were a mystery to the Afghans, something unprecedented—something of incredible proportion—was clearly underway.

On December 24, 1979, the last gunshot echoed through the streets, and high over Kabul, the cold rays of early morning glowed red on the frozen Hindu Kush.

And as the rebels escaped to untold hiding, and the soldiers tugged at their dead of crumpled with their guns, besides a ravaged building, and as civilians sat in dark rooms and furrowed their brows and children cried out in restless nightmares, perspiring in the chill, the sudden, ominous drone of turbojet engines reverberated across the glacial sky. A single hulk, an Ilyushin IL-76 Soviet transport plane, descended over the northern ridge.

The nervous chief commander at Kabul Airport telephoned Amin, who approved the landing, believing that promised help had arrived.

When the Ilyushin landed, dozens of armed Soviet troops and two airborne tanks emptied onto the strip. Within seconds, the airport was stormed and captured. Five minutes later, another Ilyushin landed.

Five minutes later, another. Tanks and troops by the hundreds swarmed into the city, and the transport planes continued to land, empty their payloads, and taxi away. Soon, hundreds of airborne tanks and captured T-62s and T-64s, with thousands of Soviet troops, patrolled the streets of the capital in an endless cavalcade.

Scattered units of Afghan soldiers, whose commanders had diligently refused to disarm, hurried to strategic points around the city and bolstered their positions.

Frantic messages reached Kabul from the Amu Darya (Oxus River): "The Russians are coming."

But no one understood why they were coming. Amin himself was confounded. Rumors flared.

The days were wrought with fighting; the nights enraged. Mujahid attacks intensified. Afghan units were struck and retaliated. And the transport flights continued without a pause.

It was a full-scale invasion. Eager to avoid repeating the ineffectiveness of the United States in Vietnam, the Soviets deployed almost four thousand tanks and armored vehicles; five hundred fighter bombers, reconnaissance aircraft, and assault helicopters; and more than eighty thousand troops. Following occupation, the numbers increased. The mass of these divisions was mobilized over land to seize Afghanistan's major cities, thundering along roads built by Soviet workers, who had been employed long ago by King Zahir.

For four days and three nights, pockets of Afghan soldiers resisted, and on the night of December 27, Aslam Watanjar emerged from the Soviet embassy compound (where he, Mazdooryar, and Gulabzoi had taken refuge) and was carried by tank convoy to the Radio Kabul station, where one Afghan unit continued to hold out. The tanks halted at a distance to avoid the conflict. Watanjar hurried into the fighting, and the Afghans, seeing their former defense minister coming, ceased firing for a moment to allow him safe entry into the building. Those inside and those defending the face of the building were appealed to and told, "Our revolution is continuing." They surrendered. Those at other points around the building couldn't hear Watanjar and were dealt a terminal blow. The radio station was captured.

At 8:00 p.m., December 27, 1979, radios throughout Afghanistan tuned to Radio Kabul for its regular broadcast. Tonight, however, Radio Tashkent, from the capital of Soviet Uzbekistan, had increased its power and was broadcasting on Radio Kabul's frequency.

As on every night, a man speaking Pashto announced the Radio Kabul news hour (half an hour of news in Pashto would be followed by half an hour in Dari). But tonight, the customary speech announcing a coup would proceed in a voice vaguely yet startlingly familiar. It was Babrak Karmal. He declared the overthrow of the "bloodthirsty agent of the CIA" and earnestly implored every Afghan to cooperate with him in dismantling Amin's "imperialist" government.

Amin, meanwhile, sat ignorant at Darul Aman, which had been surrounded by Soviet forces, whom Amin assumed were there to protect him—a strange concept, as the forces faced inward at Darul Aman.

Finally, at 10:30 p.m., enclosing Soviet troops, after hours of negotiations with the forsaken Democratic Guard, opened fire.

The fated battle raged for hours. The Afghan soldiers were valorous and proved themselves worthy of their assignment. But just before midnight, Soviet tanks turned 125 millimeter guns on the old palace, and the terrible Hind helicopters came in swift approach. A quarter of the building was blasted away, the Guard was inundated, and an elite Soviet commando unit stormed the structure.

In the very early morning of December 28, 1979, Amin was killed, along with most of his family members.

When daylight came, Babrak Karmal was brought to Kabul and installed. The Soviet conquest of the remote land called Afghanistan startled the entire world. The security of almost every nation was traumatized. (World reaction will be discussed in the next chapter.)

Moscow probably expected the Afghanistan scenario to be similar to Hungary and Czechoslovakia, where the revolts were crushed in a matter of months. Perhaps they overlooked the topography of Afghanistan, so favorable to guerrilla warfare. Perhaps they overlooked the religious fervor of the Afghans, whose highest sanctity is martyrdom. The Soviets soon realized that the Bear had met the Lion, and a long and bloody war was to follow. A schedule of creeping movement and gradual subjugation would be adopted—first, control the capita; then, the provincial capitals; then, the airports, the highways, and the bridges; and finally, the wild frontier. At least, that was the plan.

Meanwhile, months passed,. Nightly, the rebels battled the Soviets and the Afghan soldiers, who were subdued and demoralized, and whole districts were frequently controlled solely by the insurgents, who were an unpleasant shock to the virgin Soviet troops.

Moscow's army, in fact, encountered a dilemma—often sheer defiance in almost every non-Soviet in Kabul, including most of the Afghan Communists, who deeply resented the insinuation that they had asked Moscow to overrun and occupy Afghanistan. By February 1980, two thousand Khalqis and Parchamis had relinquished their positions in the regime and renounced the People's Democratic Party. The remaining three thousand feuded more vigorously than ever, crippling the Soviet campaign, particularly in Kabul, where hundreds of grudging and well-armed Khalqis and Parchamis were jostled into a single work space. Internal assassinations were common.

The capital was in turmoil. The first item on the Soviet's schedule was farther from subjugation than when it first had been seized.

On the icy night of February 22, in the antiquated Shoor Bazaar of Kabul, a gathering of Afghans stood and talked about God. "Allah-hu-Akbar" (God is the greatest) was murmured. "Allah-hu-Akbar," others repeated. Others standing nearby also returned, "Allah-hu-Akbar." Across the old bazaar, people began to gather. Many closed their eyes or watched the frosty heavens, saying, "Allah-hu-Akbar!"

The mysterious unison voices were heard in other parts of the city—"Allah-hu-Akbar . . . Allah-hu-Akbar!" What strange happening was this? Hundreds shouting to God! Should it not be aided?

Russian soldiers, sleeping or waiting in their barracks, heard the distant symphony, and soon voices all around them shouted, "Allah-hu-Akbar!"—God is the greatest!

Central Asian soldiers, sent by Moscow, heard the forlorn cry of their sorrowed homeland. Some stared down the darkened streets and whispered, "Allah-hu-Akbar."

Afghan soldiers stationed under canopies watched as thousands came out into the night, climbed onto flat rooftops, and shouted across the capital or at the glistening stars, "Allah-hu-Akbar . . . Allah-hu-Akbar!" Many troops exchanged glances or looked boldly at their commanders as they joined their countrymen in this grand reveille.

Soviet advisors and generals stared with hard eyes through foggy windows. Foreign diplomats from every non-Warsaw Pact nation went outside or onto embassy rooftops to watch the spectacle.

Hundreds of thousands of men, women, and children throughout Kabul and in the outskirts joined together in the single cry of glory to God. And when the misty rays of dawn spread over the eastern mountains, all bowed down to pray.

When the wintry sun emerged on Kabul, the waving green flags of Islam were paraded through the capital, and almost every citizen marched through the streets, shouting, "Death to Babrak, the servant of Russia," and "Russians, get out of our country!"

By 9:00 a.m., every shop and market was closed, as more than half a million people staged an unprecedented demonstration.

When the police, now an exclusive force of Khalqis and Parchamis, appeared in riot gear, the crowds became uncontrollable. Clashes erupted in every district. Half a mile from the presidential palace, Soviet troops joined a police unit and began firing into a crowd on Mahmoud Bridge. The city slid into an uproar.

For five days and nights, Kabul was at a standstill as the fighting continued. When it was over, 865 civilians were dead.

The massacre was agonizing, but no great shock to anyone.

Though the Soviets, through Babrak, were slowing the socialist reforms in the hope that the rebellion would be reversed, not a single Afghan took notice. Instead, the Soviets consensus were that the reforms would simply be better enforced by a vastly more powerful army than the previous governments of Taraki's or Amin'shad employed. These consensus were proven faulty and non-applicable due to the courageous resistance of the Afghan people and their long for self-determination, which has have stopped the reforms and supplanted Communism altogether. The Soviets had intervened illegally and prevented this. It was this prevention—this incredible violation of independence—that was more infuriating to the Afghans than the original infringement of self-determination that began in April 1978, when five thousand Afghan Communists invaded the autocratic lives of sixteen million countrymen.

Now, an outside force arrogantly blocked the natural progression of a weaker nation, on the preposterous excuse that they had been invited to do so. Babrak's alleged "invitation" was a travesty. At the time, Babrak was neither president nor a recognized citizen; he was a fugitive!

To the seasoned mujahideen, Babrak's regime was simply the latest development of an ailment that had begun fifteen years earlier. The

Soviet invasion was merely the colossal escalation of a war that had been raging for years. But to any other Afghan of any tribe, any social class, or any political conviction, the occupation of the country was an outrage less tolerable that any atrocity in its long and horrid history.

The massacre of February 23 confirmed what had been suspected:; any attempt by the Afghan people to express the *real* will of Afghanistan would be violently opposed by the military might of Moscow, which had its own will for its neighbor and the raw strength to impose it.

For the Afghan Communists, the intervention may have meant momentary survival and the defense of the revolution by the awe-inspiring might of a superpower. But it also meant that the resistance would be joined by almost every non-Communist in Afghanistan, and they would be better equipped and more determined than ever before. So if the Soviets ever withdrew from Afghanistan, no Communist regime, party, or individual could remain alive in the country. Two alternatives awaited—either Afghanistan would become another Outer Mongolia, a sparsely populated Soviet satellite; or it would become a free country, with its foundations in Islam.

On this scale, the war, now a *jihad* for freedom, continued . . .

In March 1980, there was renewed fighting in Baghlan, a mountainous province north of Kabul. I met with the mujahideen commander, Dr. Mya Gul, a medical graduate of Kabul University in Peshawar. He had commanded a rebel unit in a battle on the Dasht-i-Kilaqai, a high, scrubby desert in northern Baghlan, and reported the results as follows: fifty tanks and armored vehicles were destroyed, nearly 250 Soviet and Afghan troops were killed, and three Soviet soldiers were captured.

Another mujahid reported that on March 17, heavy casualties were inflicted upon the Soviets in the Pul-i-Alam region of Lugar Province, south of Kabul, where low but plentiful mountains provided a fast retreat for the mujahideen.

Further south, in Ghazni Province, the disillusioned soldiers of Ghazni Division revolted and, with nearby rebel forces, attacked loyal Afghan and Soviet soldiers, killing nearly all of them. In reprisal, the Soviets bombed and strafed not only the rebels and the defected division but the city of Ghazni as well. Hundreds of civilians were killed.

Ghazni Division had deserted because of such tactics. Thousands of civilians throughout the province had been needlessly murdered in the Soviet campaign, which was increasingly less concerned with adjusting Amin's reform program and more concerned with bringing a dissident population to its knees.

An *alem*, a religious scholar, who had joined the exodus of refugees and fled from Ghazni to Pakistan, reported that in his area, near the town of Maqor, Soviet soldiers had seized a copy of the Holy Quran and made it the subject of their Kalashnikovs. Since the Quran in these regions is unbound and its precious pages shared by a single community during Friday prayer, the village was left with only its recitation, by those who knew it. All were thankful that their place of prayer was left intact. Later, however, Soviet air raids targeted and demolished a number of mosques.

On a visit to Parachinar refugee camp—a despairing flock of tents sprawling across the cruel sands near Peshawar—I spoke with an *alem* (priest) from Konar Province. He said that he had heard that Muslims in Bukhara and Samarkand were forbidden by Moscow to read or recite the Holy Quran, but he had not believed it. Then, he related tearfully, one day in his village, Soviet soldiers entered the village school, beat the teacher severely, and dispersed the frightened young children who had been studying there. The parts of the Holy Book were snatched away, not to be seen again. The priest confessed that in his old age, he could not forsake the scriptures, so he had left his home and come to the desolate camp, where at least there was Islam.

From every province came reports of Soviet advisors and troops ordering the abandonment of the Quran, whose words they rightfully perceived to be the spirit of the resistance. The Quran commands all believers to "Fight those who neither believe in God nor in the Last Day . . ." (S. ix 29). This applies when the faithful are persecuted by unbelievers. "Those who believe, and adopt exile, and fight for the Faith in the cause of God, as well as those who give them asylum and aid— these are all in very truth the Believers: For them is the forgiveness of sins and a provision most generous" (S. viii 74). In devotion of such passages, nearly every Afghan was in armed rebellion or providing asylum and aid to the rebels.

In reaction, the Soviets eradicated religion from every area in their constraint. From the schools, Islam was expelled. The *Manifesto* replaced the Quran. Communist thought was woven into every curriculum; liberal texts were replaced by strictly Sovietized ones; and Russian replaced English as the required language study. Indoctrination into Darwin's theory of evolution was ordered to begin at the elementary school level. Any instructor found to be condoning the doctrines of Islam was discharged. In fact, any teacher who did not join the PDPA was replaced by a Soviet. This tenet was extended to every public office.

The media, previously subject to government scrutiny, was now completely manacled. The newspapers' names had been changed to denote the idea of a new Afghanistan and were restricted to one source of information: the Soviet news agency, Tass. Most radio and television air time was reserved for boasting the achievements of the Russian Bolshevik Revolution.

In the administration, even PDPA members were ousted and replaced by Soviets, who were deemed, without exception, to be more competent than any Afghan counterpart. Where Soviet officials had once held an important advisory office under Taraki and Amin, they now dominated every sector of government and routinely instructed Babrak's policy making. Such was the mistrust for all Afghans that twenty-five hundred Soviet soldiers were regularly stationed in and around the palace, and everyone in Kabul or entering the city was required to carry identification papers. Every Afghan in the military was constantly suspected, and the Defense Department was run exclusively by Kremlin officials. All orders and commands were issued by Soviet generals.

The integrity of the motherland was vehemently raped, and it was understood that any hope of retribution, any hope of freedom and liberty, lay with the rebellion, with their countrymen, and with jihad.

By the end of March 1980, three military divisions (Ghazni, Nahreen, and Herat), four battalions (Asmar, Paktia, Wardak, and Zabul), and a multitude of units and individuals, including some Soviets, had revolted and joined the resistance. The army, which before the Saur Revolution had comprised one hundred thousand men, was now reduced to fewer than twenty-five thousand, and many of these were conscripts, waiting to desert.

To supplement the dwindling ranks, Soviet magistrates frequently raided villages and suburbs, taking boys fourteen years old and younger. Elderly men were abducted from inns and taverns or off the streets. These disadvantaged civilians would be given one week's training and then sent off to combat, where many would die, and others, given the chance, would escape and join the mujahideen.

The greatest repercussion of desertion was the loss of military equipment to the mujahideen, so most Afghan units were disarmed and posted inside vulnerable mud-brick fortresses in the frontier. Those disarmed in the cities stayed in their barracks.

Meanwhile, the mujahideen held the entire frontier and most cities. The Soviets controlled the cities of Kabul, Kandahar, and Jalalabad (the capital of Nangarhar Province) but only during daylight. With the darkness came the mujahideen to attack, with as much success as before the invasion.

The uncanny endurance of the resistance was disorienting to most of the Soviet troops, who had been conditioned from infancy to accept and believe that Soviet victory was inevitable. The Hungarians, the Czechs, even the Nazis could not resist the predestiny of the Soviet state. Now, the USSR's mightiest machine of space-age technology and cult nationalism was being held captive by scattered bands of turbaned tribespeople, who often brandished only Enfields, or swords, or sticks and stones. Marx's ultimate society was held in check by people who were scarcely out of the Middle Ages.

Though a significant mujahideen headquarters existed in Iran, the merciless deserts and massive Soviet forces (positioned toward the Persian Gulf and Indian Ocean) in Afghanistan's west and south thwarted its effectiveness, so most insurgents from that area operated from the east, where the mountainous Afghan border is more reliably safe to cross. Moreover, most families had fled to camps in Pakistan, where they were accessible to world relief organizations. Most important to the struggle was the availability of arms and equipment in Pakistan, the port of a clandestine arms supply line from the United States, China, Saudi Arabia, and others, though only a few weapons actually reached mujahideen headquarters, the majority being siphoned by corrupt officials along the route. Most weapons used by the rebels were captured from defeated Communist forces, but it was in Pakistan where they were either redistributed or sold to enterprising black marketers. The black market operated throughout Pakistan's "wild west," particularly in Darra, where Enfields and Kalashnikovs were replicated by the thousands and sold to Afghans or smuggled to Amritsar, in India's Punjab, where Sikh extremists fought for a separate state. Many Afghans prospered in the outlawed commerce and invested all their gains in war against Afghan Communism.

By the end of summer 1980, Soviet generals decided that conclusive subjugation would not occur until the traffic between Afghanistan and Pakistan was stopped, and this could be achieved only with the capture and repression of all of Konar and Nangarhar Provinces, hosts to the Khyber and other strategic passes.

In mid-September, a fifth of the entire Soviet occupation force was deployed on the Kabul-Jalalabad highway, which climbs eastward through the Darya-i-Kabul to Laghman Province. Once past the excitable weather of the valley, the ground column was to be joined by air support, disband, and infiltrate the provinces. The preliminary units approached confidently the treacherous Mahipar Pass, where the cold winds of Siberia are sucked violently over the southern flank of the Hindu Kush toward the hot plains and jungles of the subcontinent—and where a contingent of mujahideen waited in ambush.

A sudden onslaught momentarily overwhelmed the convoy, but relief was close behind. Regardless, the accustomed air support would not come. The best-piloted helicopter would be obliterated in the tempestuous gale, so no such decisive tactic would hinder the mujahideen. The battle raged for nine hours. When it was over, and the rebels had disappeared beyond the high, dark, icy reaches, a shorter convoy resumed. The rear units struggled through a wreckage of seventeen gutted trucks, thirty-five tanks and armored vehicles, and the bodies of dozens of lifeless comrades.

Frustrated air commanders avenged themselves with a multiple sortie of twelve gunship helicopters, ordered to bomb and strafe the lower habitats of Surkhakan, the region of the Laghman Pass. And a new method of retaliation was introduced: biochemical warfare.

The perverse implications of dropping deadly substances and their horrifying effects on the human body prompted the Geneva Convention to ban their use after the horrors of World War I. As of that day, Soviet conduct in Afghanistan was not only monstrous and cruel but globally illegal as well.

A mujahid who witnessed the siege on Surkhakan reported that rebel positions and nearby villages were bombarded with explosives and several shells that simply burst on impact, incinerating a ten-meter radius and releasing a fog of bluish-green gas. Those exposed to the vapors buckled in nausea. Shortly, they began vomiting violently and then experienced wracking pain that preceded death. When the brackish haze finally drifted upward to lonely peaks, and a clear breeze washed over the landscape, 120 people—only twenty-three of them mujahideen—lay dead in fetid puddles of body fluids. Every corpse was black-and-blue and swollen beyond recognition.

News of the inhuman fate of the Surkhakanis was carried in every direction, and to the northwest was carried a forewarning that Soviet forces were approaching, en route to Konar.

The villagers of Laghman, Surkhakan's host province, were poorly armed but resisted fiercely nevertheless, successfully eluding the troop and convoys that filtered through the valleys. Scouts would warn of Soviet advances up a particular valley days before the convoy's arrival at the village. The inhabitants would scurry to hide in caves in nearby cliffs and then would return to their ransacked homes when the convoy had passed. Many villagers banded together and trekked ahead of the convoys to perch above the narrow ravines and steep passes and wait in ambush. Hundreds of villagers died battling the Soviet campaign across Laghman.

Heavy casualties were repaid to the Soviets in Alishang, a precarious valley that climbs northwest from Mehtar Lam, a town close to the Kabul-Jalalabad highway. The Soviet objective was to entrench a permanent occupation force that would block passage for the mujahideen from Nangarhar into Afghanistan's northern provinces. Instead, an insurmountable rebel attack forced a hasty retreat.

For two days, dead soldiers lay forgotten on the rubbled slopes.

When a small detachment of mujahideen returned to the battle site, scavenging birds already had begun their sordid work. It was a rare opportunity. With caution, the men trotted down the mountainside toward the naked deformity of mankind, the shameless exhibit of the truth of war.

The men wandered among the dead soldiers for several minutes before searching the blood-stained coats for the documents and identification papers collected by mujahideen headquarters. From one pocket was drawn the first item of what would become a lengthy file: the identification papers of a Cuban soldier. There had been accounts of Cuban and East European troops seen in Nangarhar and Kandahar Provinces, Now, there was physical evidence.

On the fringes of the haunting scene lay another soldier—a Russian, nineteen years old, his boyish face now ashen and his thirsty eyes a void. Deep in his pocket was a letter, its creases worn from the reading on countless lonely nights. It read:

Dear Sasha,

I am greatly missing you. Never a moment passes when my thoughts are not focused on you. Laya is now in the snow-clad mountains north of Groseen. The rigors of winter are intensifying with each passing day.

I am busy with household chores all the day long. Who knows when you will come home? Mom keeps herself busy. Keen to know the war situation, she turns to the television or tunes in the radio.

Viktor's body arrived here from Afghanistan a few days ago when it was raining heavily. Poor Viktor was married to Nadia hardly a month ago. I pity poor Nadia. How soon, this death benighted her life? I hope you will return soon.

Need I tell you how deeply I love you, how I am always thinking of you? When will you come home, my love? . . .

Her husband would return to her, and she would bury him in the cold winter. The Afghans weren't the only victims of Kremlin decisions.

At last, the battered Soviet convoys reached Konar. It was a bitter success. Weeks of trial in Laghman yielded utter futility in Konar, where the clamber north toward the highest peaks in Afghanistan was relentlessly frustrated at the end of every afflicted five-mile stretch, where groups of well-armed mujahideen invariably waited.

The Soviets avenged themselves with an air strike on Konar's Nengalam region. In the Bajawar refugee camp Peshawar, I met with Provincial Commander Kashmere Khan, the same Kashmere who led the mujahid attack on the Communist forces in Karhala during Taraki's regime. Commander Kashmere reported that the siege on Nengalam involved nine Hind gunships that, during bombing and strafing, dumped a chemical on mujahideen positions. Exposure caused vomiting, respiratory difficulty, and incapacitation. A wet handkerchief over the face brought relief, so the chemical was probably a riot-control agent, used to disable those exposed, as well as those not exposed who are prone to be distracted from the battle by a victim who is alive and needing help.

In Chaghal-Sry region, the Soviet campaign in Konar met final defeat when bands of rebels dislodged several enormous boulders and sent them crashing down the mountainsides onto an indispensable column. Scores of soldiers were crushed, and hundreds of others were trapped in a furious crossfire. The column was lost. Grieved Soviet generals decided that Konar would not be conquered until a firm base of operations existed in its southern neighbor, Nangarhar. If Nangarhar could be captured, a solid front would be launched against Konar, and the Soviets would gain control of the most critical corner of Afghanistan.

Conflicting feelings of boldness and uncertainty accompanied the Soviets' march across Nangarhar toward their geographic archenemy, the Khyber Pass. It was, of course, a race. If the mujahideen in Pakistan could rally an extensive force in the Sorkhrud region between Jalalabad and the Khyber, Soviet victory would be far from guaranteed.

When the day light spread over Jalalabad, the Soviets' tenacity was rekindled. Ground forces would rendezvous here and be redeployed with air support to take Turkhum (the Afghan name for the Durand Line Border).

After a brief rest in the prostrate city, the Soviet legions ventured into Sorkhrud. The barren highlands of jutting rocks and chasms and watersheds thundered with the awesome presage of thousands of tanks, armored vehicles, trucks, heavy artillery, gunship and transport helicopters, and troops.

In the upper realms, the mujahid outfits of local commander Ahmad Hijrat had been with little hope, until the arrival of several well-endowed pack trains and several hundred well-armed mujahideen under the command of Adam Khan (Ata Gul), the eminent hero of the mujahideen in the east.

With the courage and ferocity so vital in the Afghans, the mujahideen forces advanced down the mountains toward the invading army.

The battle that ensued would win renown. For three days and nights, Sorkhrud was virtually engulfed in blasts and fire, valor, and death. Scores of mujahideen were martyred, hundreds of soldiers died, and hundreds were wounded. A tank and three armored personnel carriers were captured and many others destroyed. Two Hind gunship helicopters were shot down. Two young Soviets were taken alive. And at last, the Soviet army retreated, leaving Laghman, Konar, and Nangarhar, except Jalalabad, as they had been before the campaign. They would stay in Jalalabad, controlling the functions of the city during daylight.

At the beginning of 1981, twenty of Afghanistan's twenty-nine provinces were completely beyond the control of the governments in Kabul and Moscow, and most were beyond even the imperiled military. Of the remaining nine provinces, including Kabul, only the capitals were under significant control, but even this control was endangered.

Early in spring, in the Chaman-i-Hozori District of Kabul city, a top Soviet military officer and his bodyguard were dragged from their jeep and killed. Their executioners escaped.

In April, mujahideen forces, probably from the nearby Panjshir valley, struck Bagram Air Base, destroying two MiG jets—an encore of the attack on Bagram before the invasion.

Following was an attack on Macroroyan, a Soviet-built complex that housed hundreds of advisors in Kabul. Eight soldiers were killed, and the central heating plant was destroyed.

Next, Tapa-i-Tajbeeg, the largest ammunition dump in Afghanistan, was raided and set ablaze by the mujahideen, unleashing staccato explosions that engulfed the entire depot and startled all of Kabul, ten miles away. The arsenal burned for two days, and its loss cost the Soviets the equivalent of several million US dollars.

As the spring solstice arched higher and the melting snows released the sleeping mountain passes and highways, the roving vehicles of war resumed motion. Fighting was renewed in Badakhshan, Takhar, Kunduz, Samangan, Baghlan, Laghman, Konar, Nangarhar, Parwan, Bamian, Maydan, Lugar, Paktia, Ghazni, Kandahar, Ghour, Herat, and Badghis. The capitals of Bamian, Ghour, and Badghis were taken and held for several days by the Mujahideen. The capital of Herat again saw fierce battle, as did the Helmand Valley in the south, near the deserts of Rigestan. Kandahar City, once firmly under Soviet control, was attacked and divided; the mujahideen occupied the old city, the Shari-Kohna.

Outside Kabul and a few provincial capitals, the only regular Soviet movement was on the major highway circuit, but this too was under siege, so supply convoys were accompanied by tanks, artillery units, and sometimes gunship helicopters. But since even a military convoy was easily ambushed, no supply convoy was, by any means, safe. A military convoy passing through the Enjeel region was finished when an assault exploded from the surrounding forest; the assailants were too well hidden to be counterattacked. Much of the convoy was lost, and what was left turned back. The Kandahar-Herat highway was closed for the next five days.

On April 12, a protected supply convoy of ninety-five trucks, carrying food and ammunition to the Soviet forces garrisoned in Ghazni, was ambushed in the Shah Joy area, a mere twenty-five miles outside Kandahar. Though embattled, the convoy refused to halt, and much of it escaped, leaving behind a wreckage of two jeeps, five tanks, eight armored vehicles, and seventeen supply trucks. Thousands of AK-47 rounds and fifty tons of food (mainly wheat and flour) were loaded onto mujahideen pack trains. Later, the civilians of Shah Joy, hiding in bushes and trees, were bombed and strafed.

On May 17, a convoy on the Kabul-Kunduz highway was attacked on the Dasht-i-Kilaqai desert. Eleven armored vehicles, eighteen tanks, and twenty-six trucks and jeeps were destroyed, and the Dasht-i-Kilaqai was named the "Grave of the Russians." Ten days later, the exhilarated mujahideen attacked a Soviet unit stationed in a sugar factory near the Dasht-i-Kilaqai. Two tanks and a personnel carrier were destroyed; thirteen Soviets and twenty-five Afghan soldiers were killed. Seventeen mujahideen were injured and six others martyred.

An important link, both for the Soviet invasion and the supply route, was the Salang Pass tunnel, contracted with Moscow in the 1960s as a development project and chiseled with foresight by Soviet crews. The three-kilometer tunnel vents an otherwise impassable colossus of the Hindu Kush and connects Kabul with the northern towns of Mazar-i-Sharif and Kunduz, as well as with Soviet Central Asia. On August 15, a band of mujahideen discharged several explosives inside the Salang. Much of it collapsed, and the Soviet lifeline to Kabul was halted for weeks.

Another element eluding Soviet control was the prisons. Kabul's Pul-i-Charkhi, the nation's only high-security penitentiary, was usually jammed with twice its intended capacity of man, woman, and child inmates, so most "suspects" were imprisoned in frontier jails, whose only barrier was a twenty-foot high mud-brick wall and a few sentries. The centuries-old warden method was rudimentary, with each guard yelling "*khabardar*" (awareness) every few minutes, to assure the other guards and the captives that he is awake and alert. Nevertheless, a prisoner was likely to be weakened by exposure, disease, or hunger, so prison breaks were infrequent, if they occurred at all. However, on occasion an assignment of sentries might hear the beat of horses and look beyond the enclosing wall of Rodat Jail to see a band of mounted rebels approaching fast, waving swords, rifles, and Kalashnikovs high above their heads. There would be a clash, the sentries would die, and the liberated captives would join the mujahideen ranks. In this way, my younger brother Salim-u-Rahman joined the resistance and later commanded several rebel units.

A more dramatic liberation occurred at Khanabad, the capital of Kunduz Province, where a contingent of mujahideen, under the command of Muhammad Sarwar, had twice engaged the sentries of the central jail without success and attacked for the third time in nine months. This time, they would confront a force of Soviet tanks and soldiers. In Peshawar, I interviewed Commander Sarwar, who gave the details of the battle. Amid the exchange of fire, mujahideen, shouldering RPG rocket-launchers, assailed the tanks. With the tanks destroyed, there were no cannon to avoid, so the mujahideen were able to move in. Finally, the main entrance was rocketed and blasted away, and the surviving soldiers fled. The operation was over in less than two hours. Of the 135 mujahideen involved, three were wounded and one died. It was a tolerable price for the freedom of twelve hundred men, women, and children.

The victories and the timeless bravery of the resistance have been preserved in the lore of the Afghans and will stand forever as a testament to their dauntless spirit. But no victory has won the immortality of that won by the Panjshir resistance in 1982. It is the stuff that legends are made of.

The Panjshir River, with its source among the loftiest peaks in Afghanistan, plunges for seventy-five miles through a gaping rift that splits the southern flank of the Hindu Kush like a wound and forms the Panjshir valley, which opens onto a broad tableland that spans sixty miles south to Kabul. Bagram Air Base and the Kabul/USSR highway skirt the mouth of the valley. The Panjshiris, mainly Tajik, gained international distinction in 1975 when they revolted against the local Daoud-installed government, overran it, and governed themselves for two weeks. Daoud's embarrassment was avenged by a brief air strike that retrieved power.

The Soviets enjoyed no such redemption. Shortly after the invasion, Kabul dispatched an operation to subdue the valley, whose inhabitants, after the fall of Daoud, had moved further from the control of the central government. But the Soviet's attempt at control was no more successful than Taraki's and Amin's attempts. Panjshir, an embarrassment to Daoud, was a humiliation to Moscow.

In 1982, after six attempts at conquest by Moscow's armies, Panjshir was a stronger, more confident, and better-organized independent Islamic republic than it had ever been. It had its own governor, courts, revenue offices, schools, trade economy, intelligence network, and mujahideen training camps, with steady traffic between the valley and the other provinces and Pakistan. Similar autonomous areas existed throughout Afghanistan, but with its diplomatic media connections with the Western world, Panjshir became representative of the whole—and a festering sore on the Soviets' "secret" war.

On May 17, 1982, Moscow launched the largest offensive to date in Parwan Province. Almost a fourth of the Communist forces in Afghanistan converged at the mouth of the Panjshir valley and commenced an extraordinary blitzkrieg. Thirty thousand troops, three hundred tanks and armored vehicles, sixty-five MI-24 Hind gunship helicopters, and 120 MiG fighter bombers and FU-25s (an experimental, tactical fighter bomber) penetrated far into the valley and laid siege to nearly every village and rebel stronghold (nearly all of which had been deserted, their inhabitants fleeing to latent hiding caves or the mountains). For four days and nights, the Soviet and Afghan forces stormed every vestige of life. At last, they were satisfied. The last Panjshir rebel disappeared beyond the crags of the Hindu Kush; all was ruin, conquered, and silent.

The occupation force was sent into the valley, accompanied by one thousand young Communists who were to instruct the villagers in proletariat duty.

Meanwhile, the rebel forces, guided by Commander Ahmad Shah Massoud, had fled Panjshir and rallied with the mujahideen assemblies in neighboring valleys. With the blitzkrieg passed, they began an unprecedented operation.

When the full length of the occupation column was well inside the Panjshir, the stretch of road and bridges leading into the valley was blown up, completely isolating the ground forces inside.

From the mountains, side valleys, and passes, the Mujahideen advanced, falling upon the Communist forces as a lion pounces on

71

a trapped animal. A raging battle commenced. The Soviets were given no retreat—there would be no driving out, no accepting of defeat or salvaging of surviving units; there would be no easy victory. Every Soviet in Panjshir would fight until he was dead, but mercy was offered the Afghan soldiers, and hundreds deserted, turning their Kalashnikovs and tanks on the enemy that had brought them there. Soviet Ilyushin droned overhead, dropping hundreds of reinforcement troops, but the figures plummeting beneath the red stars on their parachutes were targets, and few reached the ground alive.

Seven days and seven nights later, the Soviet Panjshir contingent was no more, and the Panjshir valley belonged to Islam.

And the Panjshir resistance was written into history. So renowned was this victory that Ahmad Shah Massoud became revered everywhere as Sheer-i-Panjshir (the Lion of Panjshir). Massoud and the battle he commanded became the subject of a best-selling fiction novel in the West, Ken Follett's *Lie Down with Lions.*

Every such Soviet loss fed the resistance, fed its territory, weapons, supplies, and deserted soldiers. Four months after the Panjshir defeat, when the Soviets launched their eighth offensive on the valley, there was no evading of the blitzkrieg, no trapping of ground forces, and no surprise attack. Instead, the Panjshiris were able to stage a frontal counteroffensive and defeat the Soviet forces on their own terms. Globally, the Panjshir victory in May was celebrated as the most remarkable battle of the war, second in magnitude only to the Khost offensive of December 1987. In reality, the scope of the battle of Panjshir was common in many regions of Afghanistan. The Hazarajat of Central Afghanistan, which sourrendered with high mountains, undoubtedly saw the grandeur of such battles.

Elsewhere, large-scale offensives were launched on more accessible regions, and reports reached the outside world. In July 1983, another massive bombardment of Herat leveled most of the villages that had been spared in Taraki's 1979 siege on the province. One hundred sixty mujahideen and thousands of unarmed civilians were killed. For two weeks, surviving mujahideen held their positions beneath the violent tantrum of the Soviet air force until, after a loss of three gunship helicopters, two MiG-23s (shot out of the sky with Dashaka anti-aircraft guns), and 180 paratroopers dead in the air, the frustrated Soviet pilots returned to their hangars.

In the same month, in the Nejrab region of Parwan Province, a substantial contingent—mainly ground forces—moved against rebel strongholds and several defenseless villages (most of whose inhabitants had learned from the nearby Panjshiris and weren't there to receive the attack). A two-week battle rendered a scandalous Soviet defeat—thirty-five tanks and armored vehicles destroyed, more than a thousand soldiers dead, and more than five hundred wounded. (A rebel contact at Kabul's military hospital reported that hundreds of wounded Afghan soldiers were ordered moved from their beds to make room for Soviet wounded.) When the Nejrab contingent retreated, one hundred women and children and a few mujahideen were dead—hardly worth the Soviets' price.

Such events were ignored by the world media, whose interest in the war had waned in recent years, perhaps from sheer boredom with a struggle that had no front and was a perpetual stalemate. In a decade of war, the Communists had gained nothing but contempt.

Certainly, the battles best reported in the West were those in Paktia Province, bordering the south of Nangarhar. Its proximity to Pakistan meant it was easily accessible to foreign journalists. As the primary conduit of mujahideen moving between Pakistan and Afghanistan's central interior and south, Paktia was strategically desirable and the arena of some very newsworthy Soviet operations. Between September 1985 and May 1986, the Soviets deployed seven major offensives in Paktia, culminating in an indecisive battle at Jaji.

The year 1986 was eventful. Babrak Karmal was taken to Moscow and forcibly retired, further agitating the anemic PDPA. Najibullah (formerly Dr. Najib, one of Babrak's allies expatriated by Taraki in 1978 and the chief of the secret police in the Karmal era) was given Babrak's office, amid much protest. The reason for his replacement wasn't entirely clear, but Najibullah had far less political clout than Babrak and was probably a more efficient puppet. Babrak's absence left the PDPA without an accepted Afghan leader. In effect, the Afghan middleman between the regime and Moscow was eliminated, and the regime's sense of identity was diluted further. It was a natural development. With no success in their war and with no progress toward victory, energy was turned inward, and the resistance permitted no outlet. In Moscow, fatigue grew, and restlessness was released on their client regime. In Kabul, days of pro-Babrak, anti-Soviet demonstrations were unleashed. What remained of ideological comradeship was deteriorating.

Late in 1986, the Soviets were looking for a solution. A new and vigorous general secretary, Mikhail Gorbachev, had ideas that seemed markedly different from his predecessors. He spoke of the war in Afghanistan as a "bleeding wound" on his country's military, economy, and international relations, a wound that must be healed before his revolutionary ideas of internal reform could begin to nurse the USSR out of its eighty-year decrepitude. He did not admit, however, that the wound was self-inflicted.

A series of typical propaganda maneuvers, wrought with characteristic Soviet intrigue, followed—calls for a cease-fire (which would only ratify the Communist government), claims of a unilateral cease-fire (pure propaganda refuted by Western journalists' eye-witness accounts of continued Soviet militarism), and eventually, calls of a coalition government. (Did they actually believe the mujahideen would agree to share power with the PDPA?)

Meanwhile, the entire war was taking a turn. In an event that symbolized not only that single moment between ascent and decline in all great wars but the final consolidation of Afghan brotherhood as well, the seven major resistance organizations united in the Islamic Alliance of the Afghan Mujahideen. Though the organizations would retain separate identities, it would no longer be a weakness. Campaigns would be coordinated, and no embattled group would stand alone. Most important, in January 1987, near the Vale of Peshawar, one hundred thousand Afghans of every tribe came together before the seven leaders and their banner-bearing cavalries and heard the announcement of a broad commission that was to plan the Islamic government that would reign in post-war Afghanistan.

All over the world, times were changing. Geo-political alignments began what would probably become the most dramatic and significant shifts since World War II. The historic rivalry between the Soviet Union and the United States was given serious reconsideration in a summit between Gorbachev and US president Ronald Reagan. It was unclear to the distraught mujahideen and all Afghans what the outcome of defrosting the Cold War might be. A treaty to ban intermediate-range nuclear missiles was staked, at least partially, in some sort of reconciliation about the Soviet presence in Afghanistan, which the United States strongly opposed. Maybe Ronald Reagan would invest everything in seeking friendship with the USSR, and the United States, which had been outspoken in condemning the Soviet invasion, would abandon diplomatic support for the resistance. Or maybe Gorbachev was an overdue manifestation of Soviet sanity and would relent and offer the long-awaited withdrawal agenda.

On November 25, 1987, the Soviets in Kabul launched a campaign with ambiguous implications. The largest offensive column ever assembled in Afghanistan rolled out of the capital to rendezvous with forces in Gardez, Paktia Province.

Since the Jaji offensive, May 1986, the embroiled battle for Paktia had only escalated—its nucleus, the garrisoned town of Khost.

Khost, huddled in a fertile valley at the convergence of five important routes from nearby Pakistan, is perhaps the most strategic point in Paktia and has been an ambition of both the Soviets and the resistance since 1979. The Communist garrison there had been under siege since 1978. A division of twelve thousand infantry was stationed in the valley in early November 1987, completely isolated from ground-supply transports.

Mujahideen, led by Regional Commander Faiz Muhammed Khan, battled the Khost Division with hardly a pause in two years and had recently captured the Gardez-Khost road in hope of starving the division into surrender. Nightly supply airlifts to the division were halted when Commander Faiz's men employed a recent introduction into the war: state-of-the-art, British—and US-made shoulder-launched surface-to-air missiles, the most profitable being the heat-sensing Stinger. This missile was designed specifically to chastise the Soviet air force. All over Afghanistan, as cautious Soviet pilots gained altitude and velocity as they tried to stay ahead of the missiles, their normally decisive air superiority lost significance. Gunship helicopters—the scourge of the Afghan psyche, the torturer of dreams—were a thing of the past.

With Khost air units permanently grounded, the three fortresses, perched intimidatingly on ledges overlooking the Khost valley, were without protection from rebel outfits on higher ledges. The fortresses were captured. One hundred thirty Afghan troops joined the mujahideen; fifty loyal Afghan and Soviet troops were taken alive.

The glory of triumph faltered when Khost resistance learned that a massive contingent, supported by a fleet of Sukhoi-25 war planes, was rolling out of Gardez. The sense of impending victory vanished when a second communique claimed that the column comprised fifty thousand troops. It was almost unbelievable. Yet it was true.

But the fate of Khost was far from sealed. Reports reached Pakistan, and the crisis was mounted. As the army advanced from Gardez, a force of ten thousand mujahideen, representing all seven organizations and under the command of Hezb-i-Islami leader Gulbuddin Hekmatyar and Etihad-i-Islami leader Abdurasol Sayaf, advanced from Pakistan and the other regions of Paktia.

Sato Kandau, the precarious pass that straddles the mountain spine between Gardez and Khost, was strangely inactive as the massive Soviet column clambered toward the plain that led to Khost. Forested slopes towered over the pass, creating an ideal stadium for a rebel ambush, but there was none. Something was wrong. The advance from Gardez was almost unchallenged.

When most of the column was through to Khost, the suspense was shattered. Posterior units, climbing over the Sato Kandau, were inundated in a torrent of blasts. Simultaneously, mujahideen contingents above Khost launched a major strike.

All the savagery that had racked the war, as madness racks a rabid beast, consumed Khost. For a moment, Khost was ground zero. Such an intense concentration of omnipotent rage could have become an irreversible bloodbath that ultimately would pull every entity of the war into a final confrontation.

There would be no such climax; there was no such energy. The seizure was fading.

Successful, the ambushing rebels had descended west from Sato Kandau and destroyed the bridges that linked the winding road to Gardez. The Soviets' column, sent to free the Khost division, was now trapped with it. Though the rebels were outgunned, they would not be outmaneuvered. No Hind would fly, and no rebel would be routed from the siege on the captive army. MiG-27s tore across the sky at four thousand feet and dropped bombs; few met their targets. Morale among the Soviet and Afghan troops was dying. After days of battle, they were losing their will to fight.

Meanwhile, for the first time since World War II, Soviet foreign ministers in Moscow and Islamabad issued periodic reports of the battle in progress. Most of what they reported was, as usual, exaggerated or false.

Moscow seemed eager to portray a startling victory at Khost, whether or not it was true.

During late 1989, I have spoken with, Qaribur Rahman Saeed, who leads the general press Press and Information for the Hezb-i-Islami's Political Committee. Saeed reported that the battle for Khost is still in progress, and that though additional Soviet-Afghan forces may somehow reach Khost, it is not likely they can stop the barrage from the surrounding mountains. Ground forces without air support are of little value in the land of the Hindu Kush. By the end of December, 1989, one thousand mujahideen and seven thousand Soviets and Afghan troops had died in the struggle for Khost. The Soviets reported 1,600 rebels killed and only seven Soviet-Afghan casualties. Moscow ought to realize such claims are preposterous.

At a time when the Soviet Union is negotiating terms for their withdrawal from Afghanistan, the Khost offensive seems an eccentric act, but Moscow's fanciful media releases and Paktia's accessibility to foreign journalists lend credence to the possibility that the Soviets are simple trying to demonstrate their military power to the world before admitting defeat and going home. Their demonstration is backfiring.

"And so dawns 1988. The end seems near."

It is a ghostly prospect, this freedom from war. We have lain down our lives on this altar, ready to die for our homeland, our religion, our families. Our land is soaked with the blood of our martyrs. Triumph will be stained with our tears.

In a hospital in Peshawar, a young man named Muhammed Mali lay in a bed. His left hand and both feet gone, victim of a Soviet mine. "I want to go back," he said. "I want to fight in Afghanistan, in the mountains, along with my Muslim brothers. I still have my hand, and I will return to the battlefield and fight to the last drop of my blood."

The Quran (sura ix, verse 52) states: "Can you expect for us any fate other than one of two glorious things—martyrdom or victory? But we can expect for you either that God will send his punishment from himself, or by our hands. So wait expectant; we too will wait for you."

Four months later, in Sorkhrud region, Nenggarhar Province, Mohammed Wali went to Allah Almighty.

6

Logic and Foresight

Beneath the celestial United Nations dome in Geneva, Switzerland, men and women of every nation assembled on January 4, 1980. The issue at hand was a resolution calling for the immediate unconditional and total withdrawal of foreign troops from Afghanistan. One hundred four nations voted in favor; only eighteen opposed. But there was a weakness in the UN charter—the Soviet Union, exercising a given right, vetoed the resolution, insisting that a tenet of the friendship treaty signed with Taraki and Amin in 1978 obligated the Soviets to "intervene" when, allegedly, the legal revolutionary government of Afghanistan was threatened by armed bands of mercenaries, mainly persons against progress in favor of the monarchy and feudalism, together with Iranian and Pakistani militia.

It would be an ongoing ritual. Every year, the general assembly's votes would overwhelmingly oppose the Soviets in Afghanistan, and every year the resolution would be killed.

Other condemnations were equally fruitless. On January 27, 1980, an Islamic conference was held in Islamabad, Pakistan. The mujahideen were invited as the true representatives of the Afghan people. Foreign ministers from every Muslim nation attended, and all but four nations—Syria, Libya, Iraq, and the Palestinian Liberation Organization—demanded a Soviet withdrawal. Moscow was accused of intentionally crusading against Afghanistan's Islamic identity.

On June 30, West Germany's Helmut Schmidt met with Leonid Brezhnev in Moscow and asked for an immediate withdrawal.

Even Soviet allies, while not candidly criticizing the invasion, would not condone it. In fact, Cuba's Fidel Castro, whose own troops were dying in Afghanistan, was known to secretly disdain Moscow's presence there.

A nonaligned conference in New Delhi in 1981, chaired by Castro, concluded with a demand for "the withdrawal of all foreign troops from Afghanistan." Only India's Indira Gandhi didn't vote on the referendum. As a Soviet ally, this is understandable, but India should remember that the same type of Soviet treaty that "obligated" Moscow to invade Afghanistan, kill the president, and occupy the country also was signed with India. And Moscow's armies are heading south.

A motive for the invasion was geo-strategy. Like the czars before them, the Soviets coveted the subcontinent. Leon Trotsky, a founding father of the USSR, said, "The road to Paris and London lies through the towns of Afghanistan, the Punjab, and Bengal." Though a regional, nuclear, and quasi-industrial power, India was greatly weakened by the ceaseless ethnic and religious separatist movements, political and economic chaos, and a continuing border conflict with China along the Tibetan frontier. India, though officially nonaligned, was de facto in the Soviet camp, but it would have little, if any, Western military protection against Soviet "intervention," and if Moscow was willing to invade Afghanistan on the frail pretext of Babrak Karmal's invitation, there was little reason to believe they would ignore the invitation of an Indian Communist, of which there was no shortage.

In Pakistan, Moscow demonstrated its ambition toward the subcontinent and flaunted its disregard for the sovereignty of weaker nations. Nearly every day, Soviet and Afghan government jets crossed the border and bombed and strafed not only Afghan refugee camps but Pakistani villages as well. A single raid could leave hundreds of refugees and aid workers dead. Since diplomatic agreements between mujahid leaders and Pakistani officials prohibited heavy combat weapons in the camps, there was no defense. Similarly, anti-aircraft equipment seldom found its way to Pakistani communities in the tribal frontier. In one instance, late in March 1987, twelve warplanes appeared over the border in Afghanistan; four of them crossed into Pakistan's Kurram Agency and bombed Teri Mangal village, destroying shops, a mosque, and a school.

One hundred five villagers, many of them children, were wounded and at least fifty-one were killed—possibly many more lay unaccounted for beneath the rubble.

On occasion, a company of mujahideen, returning rather hastily from Afghanistan, have been pursued by ground units over the Khyber Pass and well into the unsettled tribal districts of Pakistan, sometimes as far as twenty miles into the Northwest Frontier without being detected by Pakistan's military. When they were detected, the army was hesitant to act; Islamabad was eager to avoid a direct engagement between Pakistani and Soviet forces.

Instead, the incursions were quietly documented, to be presented in the annual and sterile UN tribunal. Every year, Pakistani intelligence reported scores of air and ground violations, and every year, in the absence of hard evidence (such as a downed plane or a captured tank), Moscow and Kabul readily denied the charges, and the semi-weekly invasions of Pakistan continued.

Despite the deliberate targeting of Pakistani communities, it might be argued that the incursions were primarily concerned with afflicting the Afghan resistance, whose morale was invested at least partially—in the parents, siblings, and children living in the camps. Kill refugees, kill the families of the mujahideen, and you kill morale.

But more subtle activities, such as the intrigues of the KGB and KHAD (Kabul's Soviet-trained secret service), countered the argument.

Bold Afghan Communists were selected and trained in espionage, demolition, and sabotage and were instructed to infiltrate not only Afghan villages, where they could covertly radio information to Kabul about rebel movements, but also the refugee camps and possibly mujahideen headquarters in and around Peshawar, via the flow of refugees or a staged desertion. It is believed that these agents also infested Afghan refugee communities in Asia, the Middle East, Europe, and the United States, where they could spy on and disrupt the Afghans for Kabul, as well as perform clandestine operations for Moscow (probably limited to petty intelligence gathering).

In Pakistan, their scheme was far more diabolical—they were probably the guts of a grand design (at the risk of sounding dramatic) for subcontinent domination. One of their functions, terrorist bombings, rocked urban areas and killed hundreds, from the wilds of Peshawar to the bustling seaport of Karachi. Though Pakistan's government publicly accused "foreign saboteurs"—namely, Kabul's operatives—the uneducated masses blamed the refugees. When several Peshawar children died in an ugly time-bomb explosion at a school, the refugees became the subject of anti-Afghan rioting. At least one KHAD agent was apprehended by Pakistani authorities, but details of the arrest were so shrouded that rumors were inevitable, and witnesses to the arrest thought it was an Afghan refugee. The only motive for anti-Pakistan behavior that a refugee might have would be self-destruction. If a fellow refugee discovered that the first was jeopardizing the asylum of all Afghans by assaulting the host country, the terrorist would be put to death. Even if the terrorist escaped detection, why would he risk losing his own asylum?

A product of the bombings, perhaps the most calculated, was the political casualty suffered by President Zia-ul-Haq. Zia's burden was the internal stability of a nation mad with factionalism, civil unrest, political and economic upheaval, drug wars (also blamed on the refugees, whose occasional caravans across the frontier traffic poppies to help fund the war), and a perpetual state of martial law. Benazir Bhutto, daughter of Zia's epic foe, the late Zulfikar Ali Bhutto, led the opposition movement, and her umbrella party, PPP (Pakistan People's Party), used the refugee situation and the related terrorism as a pawn in the plot to politically seize general headquarters in Islamabad. From the early 1980s, the PPP has demanded that the "Afghan deserters"—the refugees—be forced to return to Afghanistan, knowing that Zia, loyal to the hospitality prescribed by Islam, would consistently refuse. Thousands of Pakistanis, languid and wanting a scapegoat, rallied behind the PPP and released their frustrations in the party's cause. In reality, probably no Pakistani outside the echelons of the opposition movement truly wanted to shove the refugees over the border to be slaughtered, but compelling Zia to deny any demand was an effective device for constructing another reason to oppose him. He, not the refugees, was their real scapegoat. Of course, many complaints against Zia were valid, but it must be remembered that he was one man heading a nation in an unusually painful genesis, and peace and order could not be conjured.

During this genesis, the temptation to approve the PPP was strong, even for a few unstudied Western journalists. Benazir was a skilled politician, operating from the left while occasionally promoting a margin of pro-Americanism, a precarious method that predominantly resented the United States. It also was a baffling method, and this probably was no accident. The United States firmly opposed Zulfikar Ali Bhutto, who, by American standards, was a terrorist after his deposition, before Zia could capture and hang him. Benazir's own policies and convictions emulated her father's, and her pro-Americanism surely was nothing more than a device the mask the PPP's true affiliations.

These indirect affiliations could not be prosecuted, but legalities aside, they were undeniable. While Benazir played a clean game of anti-Zia politics, her brother, Murtaza Bhutto, took a more direct approach. He led the PLA (People's Liberation Army), an outlaw organization whose anarchism reinforced the efforts of KHAD. In fact, KHAD might be its cadre.

In 1981, Murtaza and a few confreres hijacked a Pakistan Airlines passenger jet out of Karachi. Their first stop was in Kabul, where Soviet officers supplied them with heavy machine guns. Their destination was Damascus, Syria, one of the USSR's closest comrades in the Arab world. With careful attention to protocol, President Zia asked Syria's president Assad to return the hijackers to Pakistan. Instead, Murtaza and his men returned to Kabul, where they were granted asylum. A few weeks later, mujahideen sources in Kabul reported that the men were in Khyrkhana District, being trained in sabotage and demolition by Soviet advisors. The PLA's terrorism continued, supported by President Assad and Libya's Colonel Muammar Gaddafi and instructed by the Soviets in Kabul.

Not surprisingly, the Soviet conspiracy extended to various separatist movements as well. Early in the war, Pashtunistan was galvanized temporarily in the hope of dismembering Pakistan and providing the resistance within their country, but the issue was buried. Almost every refugee stated clearly that if Afghanistan was won back, they would not spend one more night in Pakistan.

Moscow diplomatically and militarily supported India's claim to Kashmir and Jammu, the northern territories disputed between India and Pakistan, although the territories' own Muslim populations, while pledging allegiance to no one, most often leaned toward Pakistan.

A more parasitic movement afflicted Baluchistan in Pakistan's southern desert. In Quetta, Baluchistan's capital, a Communist party thrived, overseen by Ghaus Bakhsh Bizenjo and Khair Bakhsh Marri. Late in 1981, the Soviets conscripted thirty Baluch from Afghan Baluchistan, after intensive military training, these individuals were sent over the border to collaborate with Bizenjo and Marri. Sadly for Moscow, the conscripts didn't report to the party but to Pakistani authorities. Despite the obstacles, Zia's situation improved gradually. After the Soviet invasion of Afghanistan, the United States, in an effort to mend relations with Pakistan and balance the Soviet presence in the region, resumed military aid to Pakistan, lending some strength to Pakistan's vulnerable geopolitical position. Zia's support for the refugees won him additional military and economic aid from China, Saudi Arabia, Egypt, the USA, and others.

Domestically, Zia's popularity improved, nourished by the increasing visibility of his devotion to Islam, a devotion shared by most Pakistanis. He promoted the establishment of a caliphate to spiritually lead Pakistan and introduced Islamic principles into the nation's secular ministries. Though attention was paid to avoiding the alienation of leftists and non-Muslims, such alienation, in some degree, was inevitable. Regardless, Islam has touched nearly every life in Pakistan, and its guardian, GeneralZia-ul-Haq, and his civilian representative in government, Prime Minister Junejo, stayed in power for a longer term than was originally expected. The election, afterwards brought Islamic revival in Pakistan and impaired the prospects for Communism. All things considered, this might be inconsequential to Moscow. In today's high-tech industrial world, the road to Paris and London lies through the towns of Iran and the sea lanes of the Persian Gulf.

Petroleum and natural gas is the lifeblood of modern military and economic power. While the superpowers, the Soviet Union and the United States, are major producers, neither is entirely self-sufficient; the balance of their oil is provided by the Middle East countries, where, deep beneath lifeless sands, lie the reserves of two-thirds of the earth's known petroleum and gas deposits—a quarter of the world's total energy requirements.

Any Soviet inclination toward the region is probably not based on economic earnings. Central Asia and Siberia are abundant with oil, and Siberia's vast unproved wastelands will yield future bounties. Durign late eighties, a pipeline was completed from Afghanistan's rich Kunduz oil fields into the USSR, and Iran opened a pipeline into Soviet Turkmenia. Syria, Iraq, Libya, and South Yemen also provide Soviet oil, and very few supply routes are dependent on Persian Gulf shipping lanes.

Western Europe and Japan, on the other hand, are utterly dependent, and the strength and stability of the NATO alliance stands in this very vulnerable, unstable area. In 1986, the United States increased its naval presence in the Persian Gulf and began escorting American-flagged Kuwaiti tankers through the area to the safety of the Indian Ocean. The escorts were a response to Iranian anti-American and anti-Iraqi attacks by warplanes and speedboats on oil shipping, but an underlying motive might have been the Soviets' proximity.

According to Yossef Bodansky in a military analyst's report dated January 1983, six Soviet divisions were permanently based in Afghanistan's sparsely inhabited south and were trained for rapid mobilization to the Persian Gulf and beyond. Six permanent air bases were designed for year-round, all-weather operation. Not mentioned in the report but observed by mujahideen in the area: the air bases at Bagram and Shindand were expanded to twice their original size.

In a training exercise in September 1981, the Farah ground division crossed the border into Iran and, in less than two hours, drove more than eighteen miles, undetected, through Iran's vast Sistan area and back to Farah. Bandar Abbas, Iran's military base on the Strait of Hormuz, gateway to the Persian Gulf, is less than five hundred miles from Farah.

Of course, unless there is a conventional World War III (or unless Moscow is willing to risk a conventional or nuclear global conflict), the world need not worry that the Soviets will invade Iran without provocation, occupy the northern shores of the Persian Gulf, and threaten the oil supply. An internal element could take advantage of Iran's present instability and stage a coup, but Iran's Communist party was damned by the Khomeini's regime of revolutionary Islam, so a Soviet-friendly regime is not likely to come to power. However, if the Soviets rallied and trained enough Buluchis, a Soviet-supported Communist revolution for the independence of Baluchistan (the semi-autonomous ethnic region that spans across southern Pakistan, Afghanistan, and Iran) might be successful, particularly during Pakistan's internal chaos and Iran's continuing war with Iraq. The war would be civil and would not prompt the intervention of UN or NATO forces (though many nations would be willing to aid Teheran and Islamabad).

An independent Communist Baluchistan would rely heavily on Soviet aid and would undoubtedly grant the USSR naval bases at the ports of Ormara, Pasni, and Gwadar in Pakistan and at Chah Bihar in Iran, which is less than 250 miles from the Strait of Hormuz.

However, the United States and other NATO countries operate at least seventy vessels out of bases at Oman, Saudi Arabia, Israel, Djibouti, Somalia, Kenya, South Africa, Singapore, Australia, two bases of the coasts of Malagasy (Madagascar), and a particularly strategic base on Diego Garcia, a Maldives island in the center of the Indian Ocean, from which operates a rapid naval strike force.

Soviet perception was that the NATO alliance, with its bases, airfields, and huge fleets, along with a number of aircraft carriers, would rule the Indian Ocean. If the Baluchistan scenario materialized, that would change.

A Communist Baluch state would not only provide additional Soviet naval bases but also the warm water ports craved by Russia since the time of Peter the Great. Construction materials and cargo could be transported overland from Soviet territory via Afghanistan for the deployment of additional warships, submarines, and commercial vessels, without the seasonal arctic and semi-arctic assaults suffered by the ports on the Baltic Sea, the White Sea, the Bering Sea, the Sea of Okhotsk, and the Sea of Japan. In 1980, the Soviets made plans to double the width of the highway leading south from Soviet territory.

In reality, Moscow probably abandoned the whole fantasy within months. The invasion of Afghanistan might have made its fulfillment through Baluchistan geographically feasible, but without the cooperation of the Baluch, the plan collapsed. The willingness of most Baluch to cooperate with Moscow was illustrated in the outcome of the 1981 plot to send thirty Baluch to terrorize Pakistan. After reporting the plot to Pakistani authorities in Quetta, those thirty Baluch went to Peshawar and joined the Afghan resistance. No tribe in Afghanistan is immune to the agony of the nation as a whole, and just as no Afghan Baluch was willing to ally with the Soviets, few Baluch in Pakistan or Iran would collaborate with the torment of their brothers across the border.

As voracious as their aspirations toward the subcontinent, the Middle East, and the Indian Ocean might be, the politburo probably decided to invade Afghanistan primarily for defensive reasons. A historic longing (as well as Brezhnev's personal aggressiveness) surely prodded the decision, but most likely, the factors that made it final were the post-World War II twin paranoia about the power of the NATO alliance and an encirclement by NATO or NATO-friendly countries. A staggering conventional ability wasn't enough. A nuclear arsenal wasn't enough.

Moscow wanted infallible allies around the world—and especially along its borders—to act as buffer states. When a tiny strain of Communism infects a country, Moscow is there, supporting a coup and protecting the Communist regime at almost any cost. Leonid Brezhnev so championed this policy that it came to be called the Brezhnev Doctrine.

Outer Mongolia stands between the USSR and China's Inner Mongolia and part of Manchuria, but a long Soviet border is exposed to China. In reaction to the Sino-Soviet split and China's romance with the West, seven million Soviet troops are permanently stationed in ground and airborne divisions along the Chinese frontier. China was seeking a summit with Soviet leaders to ease relations.

In the West, the border north of Leningrad is exposed to Finland, but Finland is unarmed and friendly to the USSR. Its neighbors, Sweden and Norway, are nonaggressive, though Norway is a member of NATO. The continental East European countries buffer the West, and the barrier between the two blocks, erected by the Communists, is an iron curtain of concrete, barbed-wire, and sentries.

The gap of greatest concern is Turkey, a member of NATO bordering Soviet Armenia and Georgia. Iran, though hostile toward the West, is of almost equal concern because of that hostility; an angry United States, with a coalition of Gulf states, might decide to invade Iran, and the installation of US bases near the Soviet border could follow. Coupled with the US bases in Turkey, it would be quite a phalanx.

The Afghanistan gap was of concern, not because of its hostility toward the USSR or toward the West but because of the opposite—it was, before 1978, nonhostile, nonaligned, and neutral. The Soviet's soft Central Asian underbelly was completely exposed to NATO's air power in the Indian Ocean.

But the greatest concern in 1979 was that a Communist regime had come to power in Afghanistan and was in danger of being overthrown. At his philosophical core, Brezhnev realized that if the offensive spread of Communism was to succeed, potential client states would have to be confident that Moscow would defend their survival.

Furthermore, the threat to the Afghan client, by its very nature, endangered not only the future of Marxist imperial gains but also, perhaps, the internal stability of the Caucasus and Central Asia. It was a civil resistance, and its catalyst was Islam.

Of course, the Islamic revolution in Iran downplayed the comparatively tame awakening in Afghanistan, and Iranian ferment was far more likely to blaze across the Soviet border and excite the kin of three Iran-Soviet tribes: the Azeris, the Kurds, and the Turkmens. But the movement in Afghanistan had become a war, and its energy derived from its hate for Communism. If the Afghan rendition of Islamic revival reached the Muslims in Central Asia, a hibernating dream—a dream of freedom from the infidels—could be aroused.

Their time was the 1920s. Conquest by the czars had left them subjugated, but their culture and religion had persevered. But a new tyranny had taken Russia. They called themselves Soviets, and though they claimed to grasp a new form of democracy, a people's government of equality, they had known totalitarianism for centuries, and they could not mature beyond it. They came to Central Asia to impose total control, and unlike the Christian czars, they came also to impose atheism.

A fierce resistance ensued, and the Soviets named them *basmachi* (bandits), and history books echo the name. But they were not bandits. They were Uzbek, Tajik, Turkmen, Kazakh, Tartar, Yakut, Azerbaijanian, Kurdish, Kirghiz, and Bukharan, and they fought to preserve their culture and their religion and to restore their independence. They were defeated, and their land became the expedient of an alien power.

"The task," said Josef Stalin, "is to transform Turkestan into a model republic, and advanced post for revolutionizing the East." Uzbek SSR became such a republic. It is a model of technical achievement and agricultural prosperity. It is also a paradox, a model of non-Muslim pathology in the Muslim world. A January 1988 issue of *Pravda*, the Soviet newspaper, reported that Russian officials in charge of Uzbekistan's cotton revenues had embezzled $6.5 billion (the US equivalent) and that further profits were drawn by allowing a sort of Mafia to operate in Uzbekistan, thriving on an underground economy of drugs, gambling, prostitution, and murder for hire.

Unfortunately, the Soviets weren't the only offenders. We see the gangrene of Western influence in Beirut, Lebanon, where elements of Western culture try to merge with militantly traditional Muslim society and cannot.

And Israel stands as an unwelcome monolith in the Arab world, while the Palestinians carve an existence on the outskirts of their land, persecuted and pseudo-citizens, without decent rights or voice. Israel is a gift of the West. Islam must accept that its truest friend is itself, and while relations with the West, Africa, and even China are possible, even desirable, the Muslim world has a duty to itself to protect its ethics and its morality. And it has a duty to other nations. Once it was the axis of civilization, and it was peaceful and wise, but the barons of war came, and the center of the world shifted to Europe. Its wisdom survives through the Quran, and perhaps its responsibility—its destiny—is to be united as the Quran commands and to radiate this wisdom to the rest of the world, a vestige of sanity, though insanity encroaches.

Perhaps the quintessential symbol of that insanity is found in Afghan Turkestan, in the ethereal Wakhan, where the dwellers of the sky—the Himalayas, the Karakorum, the Pamir, and the Hindu Kush—meet. There, in the soft eternal wind and snowdrifts, the engineers of Russia have built silos, armed with intercontinental ballistic missiles bearing thermonuclear warheads. These high places, once the hermitage of wise men, have become the stables of the masterpiece of fools—the cosmic venom, the jinn of the last day.

Pakistan wants the bomb to counter India's bomb. It is a symptom and example of how the tides of change wash every shore and move all peoples, and change is not always good.

Central Asia resisted a change it knew would be bad, and though their longing for liberty continued to burn, decades taught them that change was unquestionable, insurmountable, and permanent. If the Afghans taught them otherwise, Moscow might face a renewed rebellion in its Muslim territories.

Afghanistan was invaded. It was logical.

Seldom is human logic blessed with divine foresight.

By 1988, Brezhnev had died without Afghanistan, Cherenkov had died without Afghanistan, Andropov had died without Afghanistan, and Gorbachev will die without Afghanistan. Partly in response to the invasion of their neighbor, Iran and Pakistan have embraced a purer Islam and have debilitated the formerly strengthening Communist movements in their countries. Ethnic nationalists, such as the Kurds, Azeris, and Baluch, have grown wary of Soviet friendliness. Communist parties around the world have learned that the Soviet Union murdered Hafizullah Amin and that the PDPA has been forced into subservience. Soviet-Western detente has been injured, perhaps permanently; various prospective arms agreements have been forsaken; and NATO has increased its presence or influence in China, Pakistan, the Indian Ocean, the Persian Gulf, and elsewhere. Moscow's overall popularity abroad and at home has suffered greatly because of the war. They fought the war at a terrific cost, and they lost, and any future alliance with or strength in Afghanistan is now forever impossible.

And the force they fought so hard to suppress, the force of Islam, has risen far beyond their military and beyond their Communism, and it has reached Central Asia.

In 1981, a few mujahideen, including Gulbuddin Hekmatyar and me, became the bearers of an incident that was classified top secret by Hezb-i-Islami because of possible political repercussions for Pakistan, although no Pakistani knew anything about it. I reveal this now in faith that as it is my own testimony—the testimony of a mere mujahid—and as few annals of the world have trusted or acknowledged the words of the mujahideen, the incident cannot be proven to the satisfaction of Moscow, the United Nations, or anyone.

It was early spring, and three Uzbeks on an inflated goatskin raft swirled down the Amu Darya (Oxus River) for a few hundred feet, reached the banks of Samangan Province, and stepped off the raft onto Afghan soil.

They were inconspicuous as they met a group of mujahideen and appealed to join the resistance. It was not unusual. But the customary interview revealed that the Uzbeks were from the Soviet Union, and they had come empty-handed, not knowing what they would find, to help preserve the freedom of a land like theirs, which had lost its freedom. They told the Afghans that any Central Asian, given the opportunity, would do the same.

They were taken to Baghlan in secrecy, and for twenty-seven days they lived as mujahideen, fighting the masters of their own country, the invaders of this one.

Over Radio Free Afghanistan, the mobile station operated by the resistance, the three Uzbeks broadcast a report into Uzbek SSR about the war, about the truth of what was happening. It was simply to confirm what most Soviet citizens, Muslim or otherwise, already knew from fragmented information revealed by Soviet veterans of Afghanistan (who were ordered to reveal nothing). They were named *ashrars*—cutthroats—but most Soviets knew they were only Afghans, fighting to preserve their culture, their religion, and their independence.

The three Uzbeks came to Peshawar, where they would live for months in the desolate camps, where at least there was Islam. (And no Pakistani knew anything about it.)

That's where I met them.

One warm Peshawar evening, as twilight glowed yellow, pink, and purple over the distant Khyber Pass, all knelt toward Mecca to pray. The three Uzbeks knelt near me.

We prayed to Allah and praised Him and thanked Him. We prayed for Afghanistan, for our martyrs, and for our families. And as our prayers diverged to the personal—each man, woman, and child in private fellowship with God—I heard the three Uzbeks pray for their homeland, Central Asia. They prayed for its liberty.

I don't know what became of them. But they were changed men. They were Soviet citizens, and they had tasted freedom and had felt the convulsion of a Kalashnikov in their hands. They were mujahideen. Maybe they died in Afghanistan, as scores of other Central Asians died, fighting Communism as their fathers did, decades ago.

They probably went back to the Soviet Union.

7

Where Men Live Free

When men from the First World—where geography is timid and the climate is easy, and civilization can spread and change rampantly—come to the Third World, they cling to their ethics, but ultimately, if only to survive, they shed their morality. It is a techno-morality, useful in lands where luxuries persuade decency, which is fatal in lands like Afghanistan, where mountains loom unforgiving, men and mighty rivers are swallowed by the desert, civilization is restrained, and the ethic is timeless—survival, strength, courage, honor. The place, like the ethic, can never be tamed, but over millenniums, the Afghans have gradually urged the ecology of irrigation and precious soil into the wrinkled skirts of the land, and a rough civility has been nurtured.

A man not reared in the culture can never know this civility. He becomes confused, in conflict, and morally delirious, so eventually he goes home, or he succumbs to wickedness; he becomes an intelligent savage. The PDPA founders alienated themselves from their heritage and its civility, as they tried desperately to master the techno-morality of the Soviets (and to superimpose it on Afghanistan), but while the machines can be imported, the ethical bridle cannot, and so Taraki and Amin became as barbarians, with techno-war capability. They killed and acted as if there was no God.

For the Soviets in Afghanistan, the phenomenon was inevitable, just as it had been inevitable for the Nazis in Europe and the Japanese in Manchuria. The Soviets came to Afghanistan prepared to deal ruthless and

91

inhumane blows and cause the annihilation of the culture. The Soviets have far more to lose in Afghanistan than the Americans had in Vietnam, so they are prepared to sacrifice more; the Afghans, who don't have the military support the Viet Cong had from neighboring China and Russia, are nevertheless far better fighters than the Buddhist Indo-Chinese, and they too have far more to lose. There is no free media in the USSR to monitor government actions, no civil liberty to protest immorality, and all foreign media are barred from Afghanistan. By the beginning of 1988, eight foreign journalists on assignments inside Afghanistan had been located by KHAD agents, ambushed by gunship helicopters, and killed. Several of the ambushes were so illogical and overdone that it was clear that the journalists were deliberately targeted. In November 1987, state-controlled Radio Kabul announced that "certain foreign journalists who entered Afghanistan illegally to spread lies about the Communist revolution" had been terminated by the military.

A letter to the United Nations issued by the Afghan resistance on April 27, 1982, read:

> The oppressed Afghan nation sincerely hopes that the free nations of the world would remember their millions of fellow human beings who are savagely attacked by air and ground just for their love of liberty and justice and their defense of their faith and homeland. The free nations should give thanks for the blessing of liberty, and they should fulfill the responsibility history has, by chance, put upon their shoulders. From the top of the UN marble palace, the national representatives to the United Nations should watch in the mirror of their conscience and heart the scenes of massacre, bombardment, destruction, and crimes committed by the Russians in Afghanistan . . . . We invite the representatives of the UN and the guardians of truth, peace, and liberty to travel to the land of free people, which has become a sea of blood and tears and to see the Russian crimes and catastrophes with your own eyes . . . .

It was not an unreasonable proposition, but the Soviets consistently refused all but the briefest and most regimented tours by UN deputies, and those, of course, were restricted to Kabul and other urban areas where the Soviets were firmly in control and no acts of savagery were necessary. For those UN affiliates, journalists, doctors, or whoever that considered touring with the rebels, an unofficial warning was circulated by the Soviet embassy in Islamabad: go into Afghanistan without Moscow's permission and an official Soviet escort, and you'll regret it. Don't try to see what we don't want you to see.

This enforced secrecy about the war was self-incriminating, but any aroused suspicions, any wild imaginations by the rest of the world, likely underestimated the atrocities and carnage. Before the evidence accumulated, who would have guessed that the Soviets were using chemical and biological warfare? What UN watchdog would have supposed the massive campaign of terror against the civilian population? Moscow had much to hide.

They were desperate. They discovered that people share a marrow with their land, and that Afghanistan knew a certain permanence, an invincibility that foreign cultures and foreign powers could challenge but never overcome. The Afghans could not be subjugated, nor could their will to resist be quelled, so the only recourse was to make resistance impossible. The fastest way to do that was to gradually starve them out of the country, to annihilate their asylum and aid, to destroy their food and shelter, and to almost totally depopulate Afghanistan.

Taraki fathered the concept in orders radioed to his troops in the village of Karhala. Since the rebels could not be captured, the local population was slaughtered. Two purposes were served: first, it terrorized, so that maybe other villages would think twice about aiding the rebels; second, it depopulated, so that should the rebels return to Karhala, they would leave hungry.

Taraki's ultimate scale of depopulation was horrendous, but the Soviet rendition was closer to migratory genocide. In its purest form, migratory genocide displaces an entire nation or race by brute force, and a whole country is vacated so the conquering race can move in. At the beginning of 1988, nearly one-third of Afghanistan's population had fled into exile. It is the largest refugee population since World War II.

While a few families have reached the Middle East, Europe, the United States, or other areas, most of the five million refugees wait in camps in Iran and Pakistan. Mud huts have been sculpted and can shelter several families, but most camp dwellers have only tents provided by world relief organizations. Since thousands of new refugees arrive each month, there is always a shortage of tents, so often three large families must share a single canopy. The region is semi-desert, so tons of grain must be shipped to Karachi and trucked to the frontier each day, and there is still hunger. Sufficient clean water is not found. In summer, spasmodic heat waves seethe at 120 degrees Fahrenheit, and in autumn, overnight temperatures can plummet to the sub-freezing rigidity that will clench the days and nights of winter. Diseases like malaria, carried by the swarming mosquitoes in the monsoon season, and tuberculosis (festering in the cramped and frequently damp conditions) boils and spreads beyond control.

Medical facilities are rudimentary and often are too overcrowded to admit less serious cases. Sometimes, a month or more is required for a wounded mujahid to be carried out of Afghanistan on the back of a companion, and by then, gangrene has set in. If it is a limb wound, a simple amputation can spare the life, but a torso or head wound can mean complications that lead to an agonizing death. In recent years, an occasional seriously injured mujahid, capable of supervised travel, has been adopted by an organization, state, or nation with a special relief fund set up to sponsor the round-trip travel to another country for advanced medical treatment and rehabilitation. But this is the exception, not the rule, and millions of wounded Afghans face perils, not only in the long journey out of Afghanistan but also in the often unsanitary, insufficient, or outdated treatment that awaits them. It is an unavoidable condition of war, and some very capable doctors must live with undeserved guilt and frustration.

Obviously, many threatening complications could be averted if the wounded could be treated within a few hours or days of the incident, but the Red Cross and other relief organizations are forbidden, like everyone else, to enter Afghanistan. Hospitals, identified as such by international symbols emblazoned on their roofs, are deliberately bombed. A few courageous foreign doctors, mainly French, practice inside Afghanistan anyway, but the risk is high, and they must be mobile, so their facilities are usually contained in a single black bag. Their patients often require an eventual trip to Pakistan.

In the camps, the Afghans have the highest birthrate in the world, but nearly half the infants die during their first year of life.

Life here is devoid of comfort, privacy, or inner peace. The Afghans have fled into total despair. But there is some safety here, and there is some hope, and bedlam is behind. "The nightmares are the worst disease in these places," one refugee has said. "These women and children—they remember the Russians bombing their homes and killing their families." Life in the camps is preferable to life in Afghanistan.

Bestial aerial and artillery bombardments are only the beginning. The Afghan psyche fumes with ghastly scenes of more personal atrocities.

Late in August 1985, Soviet helicopters landed in Andar, a small village in Ghazni Province, and several soldiers stepped out to search for inhabitants and draft conscripts. Such recruiting typically was carried out with all the professionalism of a raid—homes were looted, animals and sometimes villagers were shot simply for sport, and the enlisted men and boys struggled and resisted but often were virtually dragged away to duty.

Andar was no different. One family tried to defend itself with a single .22 caliber British rifle. Two girls and their mother depended on the father and the twelve-year-old son for farming and other difficult labor, and of course, there was much love in the family. Visions of the man and boy being dragged into the helicopters and taken away to probably die, and thoughts of the wife and two girls trying to survive alone and in sorrow suddenly became a crushing reality. They huddled in their shadowy cottage and clung to the rifle. As the soldiers approached, the father yelled a warning and fired a few shots. Undaunted, the Soviets trotted to the home and forced the door open, one of them swinging the butt of his Kalashnikov with the opening of the door and knocking the father onto the earth floor. The old British gun was kicked across the room. One of the daughters must have dashed for the gun, because one of the soldiers shot both of her legs, and she crumpled to the floor. Paralyzed by fright, the mother and second daughter could only watch in terror as the soldiers grabbed a clump of the father's and son's hair, hoisted them onto their knees, and blasted several bullets into the backs of their heads.

Other villagers gathered at a timid distance and They watched not only their men and boys being taken but also a woman and girl, screaming and crying hysterically as a pair of stalwart uniforms hauled them into the hull of a gunship. As the Hinds lifted in a swirl of dust and noise, the veils and the raiment of the woman flailed into the dust storm and drifted softly to the earth.

Later, two miles from the village, their naked bodies were found, twisted and broken from a several-hundred-foot fall.

The Communist Afghans under Taraki and Amin were barbarous, but they were nowhere near as perverse in their enjoyment of it as the Soviets. And they never indulged themselves in the wanton raping of women and children. They murdered without dignity, but never did they violate the sexual sanctity of the Afghan female.

In the broil of the Dasht-i-Marghow desert, in July 1984, twenty Soviets and four Afghan troops drove into a village seeking water. When a woman brought a kettle of water to the Afghans (villagers often refuse to serve Soviets), two Soviets forced themselves on her while the other Soviets cheered. They were tearing off the woman's clothes when the four Afghans opened fire. Nine Soviets were killed, five were injured, and the woman escaped to her home before the four Afghans were shot. They died to protect the woman's chastity.

In every sense, the Soviet presence was far worse than were the Afghan Communist regimes. Taraki's and Amin's men once desecrated the mosques by using them to preach Communism. Soviet soldiers used the mosques as latrines and used pages of the Quran to wipe their hands.

Soviet methods of murder also were more brazen, and pleasure was derived from how inventive the method was. Perhaps some soldiers eventually grew bored and decided that cutting throats, hanging, and beheading were too conventional.

For relief, they tied up civilians, dumped gasoline on them, and tossed a lighted match. Other Afghans were forced to watch. It was a horror, unimaginable to most, to see a friend burn alive, to hear the shrill screams that die in an animal wail, to smell the burning flesh. Human flesh smells sweet. That was sweet and sour.

One refugee reported, "The Russians and their puppet regime in Afghanistan burn people . . . more than wood."

Other civilians (and sometimes mujahideen) were bound at the wrists and ankles and forced to lie in rows in the path of an oncoming tank. They were not blindfolded; the first man to be crushed was fortunate, as the others would see and hear the body being ground into the dirt, and the massive tank quickly approaching with no escape. Thirty seconds can be an eternity.

An arrested Afghan likely saw the most impressive examples of Soviet creativity. Trials were reserved for Soviets, so the hundreds of thousands of Afghan military officers, intellectuals, religious scholars, students, nomads, merchants, farmers, and others that became "suspect" and were taken into custody were simply interrogated. If the desired confession wasn't extracted, they were beaten and kicked, often into unconsciousness. When they were roused and threatened with torture, they usually confessed to whatever they believed was suspected. If they didn't, one or several of a wide variety of measures would follow—their fingernails and toenails would be removed with a pair of pliers; they would be electrocuted in a chair or on a rack or by wires taped to their testicles; their spouse or child would be summoned and electrocuted in front of them. It happened, and it was terrifying, but a confession usually brought the same fate, sometimes a worse one.

By the beginning of 1988, possibly as many as eighty thousand political prisoners had been executed or had died and rotted in dank, dungeon-like cells in the frontier. Standing before a firing squad was the official form of execution, but restless guards and wardens might devise more entertaining methods. For its irony, subtlety, and the meek crying and pleading that it induced, the sentries seemed to enjoy forcing the prisoner to dig the holes in which he or she or a spouse would be buried. Many were buried alive.

Many survived prison and were released or escaped, but often, a disoriented, traumatized life awaited them. They walked away with unwarranted amputations or sexual mutilations. They struggled with manic-depression, paranoia, or psychosis—the effects of reckless, sometimes experimental reprogramming and psychological torture.

Outside stockade compounds, Soviet targets of terror weren't particular, and sometimes an entire village or a section of a city was destroyed without internal provocation. A nearby rural or urban sniper that escaped alive was all the justification the Soviets needed. In the frontier, a community that never harbored a mujahid might return to their homes after a raid and find their cottages and fields booby-trapped—grenades rigged to explode if doors were opened or if food or firewood was gathered.

Small "butterfly mines" were dropped from Soviet planes in fields or along paths, and many regions were peppered with them. On paths frequented by rebel units, the mines were drab-colored and shaped to resemble leaves or stones or undistinguished objects. But near villages, in fields or orchards, or on hillsides, the mines were often brightly colored and resembled wristwatches or toy planes, dolls, animals, or something else likely to pique the curiosity of a young child. Afghan students of English impulsively called them "baby traps." They were designed to maim, not kill, and countless Afghan children ran giggling to play with a treasure and had their hands, feet, or portions of the face blown away. Those who survived the trauma, shock, infection, and excruciating pain may never walk, see, or hear again. Their childhood was lost, and little toys will be objects of fear for the rest of their lives.

For the civilian who remains in Afghanistan, the fear of bombing, rape, murder, torture, dismemberment, and other terrorism—the omnipresent possibility of sudden death—is constant. But for all Afghans, fear is a pliable dynamic; it can be controlled. Menace has always been a reality of life in Afghanistan, and the Afghans have cherished their homeland anyway. Soviet tactics toward depopulation have not relied on fear but rather on the possibility that life in Afghanistan can be made utterly impossible.

Vacant fields and orchards were bombed, livestock was machine-gunned, irrigation networks were dynamited, and water sources were contaminated. Protracted droughts and famines rendered vast regions uninhabitable. The entire Wakhan Corridor was depleted of life. Its population, near starvation, stumbled into Chitral in northern Pakistan. These were the same policies followed by the Soviet-backed Marxist regime in Ethiopia. The "famine" in Ethiopia was caused by driving the people off their centuries-old farms for the purpose of "land reform."

This widespread destruction of the ecology is not a casualty of battle. It is systematic—a deliberate, structured, premeditated campaign.

Irrigation in Afghanistan is not a riddle of canals, as is common in most of the world, but in an underground system of tunnels, vented by wells. In the tunnels, precious water is shielded from evaporation, and in the deserts, some tunnels continue for tens of miles. In high mountain valleys, where rain clouds seldom reach, tunneling surrogates damming, which would submerge fertile soil. Irrigating beneath a single region can require centuries of toil. Some tunnels in the Dasht-i-Marghow desert in southern Afghanistan are several thousand years old.

When Genghis Khan came, thousands of Afghans were crammed into these tunnels, and the Mongol cavalry stampeded over them until the tunnels collapsed. These tunnels have been centuries in reconstruction, and even Mohammed Daoud's administration had engineers on the project.

The Soviets destroyed the tunnels on a scale that Genghis would have admired. Originally, the intent was an expedient, as all the reforms seemed, but when the rural population saw their water supply being buried, they rebelled. The purpose of collapsing the tunnels was to stabilize the ground so that roads could be built without fear of collapse, but the plight of the farmers and shepherds, left with no way to quench their land or animals, was ignored.

The intent was malicious. When the Red Army reached a village, they often bombed the tunnels simply to afflict the people who depended on them. Occasionally, if the village was "suspect," several men, women, and children would be summoned, bound, gagged, and thrown into a well, and a grenade would be hurled after them. If twenty or more people were cast into the well, not all would die when the grenade exploded. The well would cave in, and the people near the bottom would starve or suffocate beneath the twisted corpses of their family and neighbors, alone and in darkness.

Methodic sabotage of a local ecology effects depopulation but gradually. Meanwhile, the locals may be able to subsist on debris and reserves for weeks, and the resistance may still find asylum and aid there.

Perhaps impatience prompted the Soviets to concoct a fast, efficient solution—a device that would virtually annihilate acres of field, orchard, livestock, village, and villagers in a few seconds, without the radioactive fallout that might reach the outside world and alert other nations.

At the end of 1981, over a village in Herat Province, a Soviet plane, gliding at low altitude, dropped a heavy cloud of white powder. Seconds later, the falling bale ignited, and a monstrous fireball tumbled over the village. The function of the incendiary was the same as napalm, used by the United States in Korea and Indochina, but its results were more impressive. Napalm may spare a life if the victim has the presence of mind to tear off the splashed clothing. The Soviet device offered no such opportunity. Nothing was left of the Afghan village. Even the mud-brick houses were reduced to ash.

In many regions of Afghanistan, scorched-earth tactics brought the desired outcome. In areas where the resistance was once strong, where food and shelter was once readily available, Mujahideen units remained only briefly, surviving on grass and trickles for weeks at a time until painful hunger forced a retreat.

From the beginning of the war, as if they were completely immune to international laws governing the conduct of war, the Soviets wholeheartedly violated almost every tenet of the Geneva Convention of 1949 and other international treaties signed by Moscow, which represented the global consensus on civilized, humane, and appropriate wartime behavior.

They pillaged. They deliberately bombed educational, cultural, and religious property, and hospitals, including those identified as such by red crosses and other international symbols. They employed chemical and biological warfare, including mycotoxins (which produce hallucinations, sever liver damage, hemorrhages, abortion, convulsions, neurological trauma, and death), as well as a mysterious agent that produces sudden death with no prior symptoms. They tortured vehemently. They persecuted religion. They seized hundreds of children from schools and homes and forcibly sent them to the Soviet Union for several years of education, despite the parents' protests. They invaded and attacked a nonbelligerent state, Pakistan. They did not distinguish between combatants and civilians (who were allowed to defend themselves against unlawful attack and who did not display their weapons openly and engage in combat, as the mujahideen did, as prescribed by international law). They mistreated and murdered thousands of civilians, refugees, and prisoners of war. They engaged in wanton destruction without military necessity. They needlessly exterminated nonaggressive segments of the society. And they adopted a policy of genocide—not direct genocide, as Hitler attempted with the Jews, but international law does not distinguish between direct genocide and migratory genocide. Moscow has much to hide, but nothing has been hidden.

During the course of war, dozens of foreigners each year tour Afghanistan with the resistance, and they were not wild-eyed mercenaries. While it wastrue that thousands of Mid-Easterners, Africans, Europeans, Americans (usually Vietnam veterans), South Americans, Australians, and Asians from Japan to India annually came to Peshawar like pilgrims, seeking adventure, absolution, or just a worthy cause and petition to accompany a mujahideen caravan into Afghanistan, almost all werepolitely denied, thanked, and told to pray. It is the Afghans' war, and while the world's moral support is coveted, it must remain the Afghans' war, and no other nationality should die for it, barring the incidental risk allotted those few who are permitted to enter Afghanistan. Those few are doctors, lawyers, and journalists, internationally hailed as exceptionally prestigious in their careers. And it has been their testimony, their eye-witness accounts, and their film footage that collated with and confirmed the testimony and documentation of the resistance, the refugees, and the Afghans inside Afghanistan, as well as captured Soviet soldiers (whose rare interviews with Western journalists verified Soviet tactics with no signs of duress).

The detriment to global prestige isn't the only way the Soviets suffered. Afghanistan has become a war of attrition, but it was not the resistance that eroded. Aside from the scathing defeat of the Red Army on the battlefield and Moscow's perpetual inability to consolidate any gains except the tenuous daytime control of Kabul city, Jalalabad, and a section of Kandahar city, the Soviet Union was exhausted of finances, military strength, internal security, and technical secrets. (While the testing of new aircraft, military concepts, and prototypes of weapons and systems was beneficial to Moscow, much of this information reached the West across Afghanistan's open frontier and benefited NATO as well.)

Information gathered by Afghan militaries secretly working with the resistance suggested the average daily Soviet military expenditure in Afghanistan was $2.7 million (US). An Afghan general, Abdul Shakoor Khan, who defected to the mujahideen in 1980, believes that Moscow may have spent as much as $3.7 million per day. All of the natural resources in Afghanistan wouldn't reimburse the cost of one year of occupation. It may seem an outrageous figure until one considers the cost of sustaining 120,000 troops, the cost of Soviet ordnance (for instance, one RPG-16 rocket-launcher projectile costs $1,000), and the daily destruction of APCs, tanks, artillery dumps, helicopters, and aircraft. In November 1986, Afghan pilots stationed at Shindand Air Base covertly contacted a mujahideen commander in the area and gave him the data necessary for an infiltration of the base's perimeter. When night came, a rebel unit equipped with RPG-7s successfully penetrated the airfield and proceeded to destroy twenty MiG fighter bombers, including several MiG-25 high-performance, twin-engine, all-weather air-superiority and reconnaissance fighters, and even a MiG-27 or two. Particularly expensive days such as that one explain the high expenditure average.

A MiG or SU-25 piloted by a dedicated Soviet was not necessarily safer than a MiG sitting dormant on a guarded airstrip. Engaging a rebel with an RPG and some luck—or a Stinger-armed rebel without luck—can be equally costly, especially as Soviet morale dwindled and dedication was ousted by apathy.

If an embattled Soviet soldier wasn't rife with fatigue and vacant of purpose, preoccupied with self-preservation, or listlessly awaiting the order to retreat, he was surrendering to the mujahideen or deserting with the Afghan troops. Like the Americans in Vietnam, Soviets ceased to believe in the cause. Most of them never understood the cause. When they were enlisted, they were told they would be fighting an invading army of Americans, Chinese, Pakistanis, or Egyptians. When they discovered they were fighting Afghans to preserve a small, corrupt, unpopular Marxist regime, their cause became an ugly enigma. Next, they were told the resistance was commissioned and paramilitary trained by the CIA, but most understood that defected Afghan and Soviet troops trained the rebels, and the motive of the resistance was not a pay-off from the West but a belief in freedom and a love for their homeland. For many, the Kremlin became the enemy, their commanding echelons symbolic of hypocrisy. As their buddies died, the resistance grew stronger, and the Red Army cowered in garrisons, and the mightiest military machine in the world faced defeat by a medieval guerrilla army, their purpose seemed the worst kind of futility.

Those who didn't desert resorted to delinquency. Black marketeering, prevalent in the Soviet Union, became remedial therapy in Afghanistan. Troops stationed in city outskirts and villages located rebels and rather than killing them, they bargained for trade. Throughout Afghanistan, bartering between rebels and Soviet troops was common; a few entrepreneur mujahideen who were ambitious enough to approach a soldier would supply fruit, cigarettes, transistor radios, or hashish in exchange for weapons and ammunition. In the streets of Moscow, a kilo of hash might sell to an enterprising foreign tourist for $3,000 or to a citizen for slightly less. If a soldier could trade an issue weapon and ammunition and subsequently get a kilo of hash, he made quite a profit. The Central Asian soldier's favorite contraband was the Quran, and smuggled copies circulated underground throughout the Soviet Muslim republics.

Probably not much hash reached the Soviet Union; most soldiers who bought it used it. Russian troops were the tormenters of Afghanistan, but neither was their life made easy by the mujahideen, and a fix of mild narcotic could get them through a long and grueling battle or simply through the night.

There was nothing pleasant about serving in Afghanistan, and apparently, returning home was equally barren of comfort.

An element of Soviet leader Mikhail Gorbachev's quasi-revolution of *perestroika* (restructuring) was *glasnost* (public disclosure), which warranted unprecedented news gathering and reporting with the Soviet Union and required various Soviet agencies and bureaus to release information once forbidden. The topic of Afghanistan remained officially taboo, but gradually, some of the more secure Soviet newspapers, periodicals, broadcasters, and filmmakers cautiously investigated and reported a few semi-controversial aspects of the war. Under Brezhnev and Andropov, graves of soldiers killed in Afghanistan were marked "killed in action," with no indication of where or how. Mothers and widows of these soldiers were warned not to talk about their grief. Later, Soviet bureaucracy revealed a portrait of the Afghanistan veteran.

For the Allied nations and foremost the USSR, World War II was a hero war—bad and good was black and white, patriotism reigned, and when at last the evil Axis powers were toppled, the men and women who fought were immortalized. Throughout the Free World (at that time), the dead and the living of World War II were honored in the grandest style. Celebrations, parades, eternal gratitude, and admiration welcomed returning veterans; elevated monuments deified those who had died. Elaborate war memorials centered every Soviet city from Leningrad to Alma-Ata to Vladivostok. Even decades later, no aging Soviet veteran of that war showed himself or herself in public unless fully and proudly decorated with the medals and ribbons awarded in service. Josef Stalin was a merciless tyrant. Twenty million Soviets perished, but the time spewed glory.

Time has passed. In this age of nuclear fission and space travel and awakening environmental responsibility and Third World emergence, and perhaps the dawn of enlightened technology, war is not synonymous with solution, or with a necessary season in the cycle of peace, or with glory. War has become something dirty—something deep, dark, and surreal, like the bowels of hell.

For most of the 275 million Soviets, the war in Afghanistan embodied all that was most shameful about the USSR, and returning veterans represented not pride but disgrace. These Soviet veterans could never truly go home; the people who were friends, neighbors, or even family might bitterly resent them. They faced discrimination, job shortages, and sometimes public humiliation (they were taunted and spit at). Many were crippled, paralyzed, invalids, or otherwise disabled. Despair, loneliness, chronic depression, alcoholism, and post-war shock syndromes were common among them.

Initially, veterans were not permitted to form their own support organizations. *Smena*, an official periodical, quoted one frustrated youth as saying, "In Afghanistan they trusted us with machine guns, but here they don't want to trust us with a basement room."

Many turned to crime. Others suffered fits of violence. Some became vigilantes. In Ukraine SSR, a young man yelled "Hey cripple" at a wounded veteran, and the veteran killed him with a crutch.

Harsh public opinion also found the once untouchable perpetrators. Around the world, anti-Afghan-war protesters rallied on Soviet embassies and consulates. A rare demonstration by Soviet citizens rocked Red Square in Moscow. Despite the comprehensive domestic propaganda campaign, the facts surfaced, and resentment toward the Kremlin spread. Across the Soviet Union, the war fueled civil unrest, not nationalism.

In February 1988, top Soviet officials in Afghanistan declared that a military solution to the war would be theoretically possible—if Moscow tripled its forces there, contributed a large permanent occupation contingent, and perhaps militarily sealed the border with Pakistan and extensions of the border with Iran. With all other military requirements confronting the USSR, this seemed far beyond consideration, and the top Soviet officials who issued the report also submitted a strong recommendation for a withdrawal from Afghanistan. Mikhail Gorbachev agreed.

And so, for the first time in its seven-decade history, the Soviet Union lost—and lost fabulously.

In 1983, thirteen mujahideen, armed with RPGs and Kalashnikovs, swam across the Amu Darya from Takhar Province to Soviet Uzbekistan. After crossing the passagethrough the razor-coil on the Soviet border, the men trekked several miles into the USSR until they came upon a collective farm. Two hundred seventy-five sheep were wrangled and driven to the border, where the Afghans destroyed a border post, seized a Soviet dock, and began ferrying the animals to Afghanistan. The resistance in Takhar lived on prime mutton for months.

In March and April of 1983, the mujahideen in Badakhshan Province managed several excursions into Soviet Tajikistan, where they were given asylum, food, and supplies by any Soviet Tajiks they met. Organization membership cards of various mujahideen parties were distributed throughout Tajik SSR. Several border posts and patrol officers were annihilated, and scores of sheep and cattle were rustled to Badakhshan.

Late in October 1987, mujahideen in Badghis Province crossed into Soviet Turkmenia and struck a military installation. Twenty-eight Soviet troops were killed. A few days later, rebels fired rockets across the border at a mobile unit camp, destroying a tank and an army vehicle. Hours later, they crossed the border, destroyed two more vehicles, inflicted heavy casualties, and retreated with one death and several injuries.

The Afghans in the 1970s were vulnerable to an invasion. The Afghans in the 1980s returned the gesture.

In November 1987, the Soviet Union hinted at a resolute willingness to withdraw its troops from Afghanistan. During talks in Geneva, Soviet Deputy Foreign Minister Yuli Vorontsov suggested to US Under Secretary of State Michael Aramco that Moscow might be ready to accept the formation of a broad-based coalition government in Afghanistan, to serve for an interim period, pending national elections—a coalition that would include both Afghan Communists and rebel factions. Vorontsov also said, "General Secretary Gorbachev will have something to tell President Reagan on Afghanistan" in the US/Soviet summit meeting in December 1987.

It was true. During that historic meeting, the general secretary, for the first time, expressed a definite desire for an end to the Soviet involvement in Afghanistan, as well as a new flexibility about a timetable for the withdrawal. In 1987—the year of twenty-two wars, more wars than in any previous year in recorded history—our war was finally ending.

At the beginning of 1988, the wheels were turning. In January, Soviet Foreign Minister Eduard Shevardnadze, on an official visit to

Kabul, announced, "We would like the year 1988 to be the last year of the stay of Soviet troops in your country." In statements to the press, Shevardnadze implied that the fixation of a pro-Soviet coalition was not going to be a prerequisite to the withdrawal. This startling revelation rocked the capital and sent all who were part of it scrambling to try to find some assurance of existence after the war. There were few illusions about the survival of the Marxist regime; once the Soviets left, the Communists wouldn't last an instant.

By January1988, thousands of Afghan troops had deserted and joined the resistance. Hundreds of Afghan government officials sent messages to the mujahideen, pleading safety and post-war citizenship if they were able to defect. Most replies were affirmative, but a few questionable officials were required to first prove their sincerity. They were asked to plant a bomb in Communist headquarters, send vital intelligence to the mujahideen, or something else damaging to Najibullah's regime. Fewer than two thousand officials were true Communists; the twenty thousand others—those who were not persuaded Marxists yet participated in the government—were welcome to defect and would be treated fairly and with respect. Even a true Communist might defect if his reputation was clean—if he had not personally participated in or advocated a criminal act (as defined by the mujahideen). Shortly after Shevardnadze's statement, Najibullah's brother defected to Panjshir with his family and was granted asylum with Ahmad Shah Massoud. He and his family were given safe passage to Pakistan, from where they have immigrated to the United States.

Meanwhile, Najibullah, possessed with power, frantically maneuvered to establish his own post-war domination of Afghanistan. Loyal KHAD agents in Pakistan escalated their operations, striking the exiled intellectual community in an effort to weaken the ability and cogency of the resistance. In February1988?, Syed Majrooh, a former professor at Kabul University, was assassinated at the office of his independent Afghan Information Center news service on the outskirts of Peshawar. Majrooh's death was an irredeemable loss. Fortunately, most other Afghan intellectuals were far beyond the reach of Najibullah. They were safe behind an entourage of bodyguards, indiscernible in the throngs of refugees, or on other continents, waiting, studying, and proclaiming the cause of their people to the world.

In Kabul, Najibullah's stratagem relied on political cunning, but he was never proficient in that. He wanted the Soviets to ensure his continued position of power after the withdrawal, but instead, he drew Moscow's impatience and prompted Shevardnadze to issue a warning to anyone who placed "personal aspirations above the interests of the nation." While Najibullah's Afghan comrades pursued post-war asylum in the USSR, Eastern Europe, or India, Najibullah stirred in the fever that would be his destruction. He was a sycophant and bootlicker—nothing more—and if his mirage of grandeur persuaded his puppeteers to leave him behind, his life would end.

Najibullah should have realized that the war didn't begin when the Soviets invaded, nor would it end with their leaving. As long as there was one Communist, one Muslim, and one stick or stone in Afghanistan, the war will not end. There will always be Muslims. There will always be stones. The Communists must leave.

The peace accords to end the Soviet occupation will have been signed in Geneva on March 15, if all went well, so on January 20, UN mediator Diego Cordovez began shuttling between Kabul and Islamabad, Pakistan's capital, to negotiate an agreement. All parties observed a cease-fire along the Khyber to Kabul highway. It seemed almost absurd that the UN chose to mediate between Kabul and Pakistan, rather than between Moscow and the mujahideen. Yunis Khalis, the leader of Hezb-i-Islami, and the chairman of the Islamic Alliance of Afghan Mujahideen, consistently refused to meet with Cordovez until Februar, 1988, at Pakistan President Zia-al-Haq's request. In that meeting, Khalis relayed the indignation of the resistance at having been practically excluded from the talks. "We will not abide by any settlement unless the mujahideen have a direct part in the negotiations." Fortunately, the indignation would subside as Pakistan sensitively tried to represent the objectives of the mujahideen.

On February 8, Gorbachev, in a statement carried by the Soviet news agency, Tass, announced that if an agreement could be reached by March 15, the Red Army would begin pulling out on May 15. Half the troops and advisors would leave in the first ninety days, the rest during the following six months. Indeed, the end had already begun; schools for Soviet dependents in Kabul began closing down, and these dependents returned to the USSR.

The day after Gorbachev's statement, Diego Cordovez declared that a virtual agreement on the withdrawal timetable had been reached between Kabul and Islamabad and that only "logistical, technical, and practical details" remained to be outlined. In reality, much larger problems were unresolved.

Moscow had said in January that a broad-based transitional government should serve during the withdrawal to ensure stability and accommodate a cease-fire. "We have no intention of leaving Afghanistan hanging on the skids of helicopters," Deputy Foreign Minister Yuli Vorontsov told US officials, citing the bloodbath that chased the American pullout from Vietnam. The Afghan resistance replied that while independent realities and regional commanders could not be spoken for, the Islamic Alliance and its affiliates would abide by a cease-fire. In concurrence, the chief Pakistani delegate to the Geneva talks, Acting Foreign Minister Zain Noorani, stated that agreement on the composition of the interim government must coincide with the signing of the peace accords.

Then Kabul rejected the condition, and March 15 passed with no signing.

Passions were boiling on every side. Peace was slipping away.

Although most PDPA members seemed willing to capitulate, Najibullah and a few cohorts continued to cling to their visions, encouraged by the lingering hopes of some Soviet generals. Dreams are survivalist; dreams of power and conquest can outlive the host. Gorbachev had evidently given his generals an ultimatum: win this year—or lose.

A single possibility arose. If the resistance could be impeded from a position of administration, and the United States began tapering off humanitarian aid, and the Red Army escalated its efforts, and KHAD continued its operations in the Northwest Frontier, a last-moment Communist victory, born in the vacuum of the withdrawal, could materialize.

Perhaps the idea wasn't limited to Kabul. Perhaps the planners at the Kremlin sheltered the thought as they authorized the December offensive in Khost. It was grimly conceivable in March, as turbulent fighting heated Paktia, Ghazni, Baghlan, Nangarhar, the Kandahar-Herat highway, and the old Muhallahjat section of Kandahar City. No Afghan army units were involved. The Red Army was in frenzy.

Meanwhile, Moscow's and Kabul's representatives to the Geneva talks angled to prevent the formation of the interim government from being tied to the withdrawal agenda. Instead, they revived their earlier demands that the United States should cease all aid at the beginning of the withdrawal and that Pakistan should refuse any further accommodation to the mujahideen. They reasoned that these measures would ultimately force the resistance to resign, hence securing peace and diverting a potential civil war when Soviet intervention ended. An interim government would, of course, serve the same purpose, but to link the appointment of an acceptable administration to the accords would only delay the withdrawal.

Pakistan maintained that only a broad-based government could satisfactorily affirm the withdrawal, guarantee compliance to the accords, and oversee the safe return of the five million refugees.

It wasn't unthinkable that Moscow would pursue an elusive last chance. If the Afghan Muslims had been permitted to defeat the Afghan Communists prior to the Soviet invasion, the internal security of Central Asia would have been threatened. Now, if the Afghan Muslims managed to not only vanquish Afghan Communism but drive out the Soviet army as well, the security of all of the Soviet Union and Eastern Europe could, theoretically, be endangered. In the same way the Afghan defeat of the British heartened India and intrinsically heralded the fall of British colonialism, the Afghan defeat of Russia could be a glimmer of destiny. Though the prospect was remote, no empire is forever, and the uprisings in the Crimea, sparked by nationalist tensions between Christian Armenia and Muslim Azerbaijan, illustrated that the Soviets were not as in control as once believed, and they were keenly aware of separate national identities. Non-Russian soldiers serving within the USSR were always stationed far from their own republics, so if unrest erupted in their own vicinity, their loyalties would be to Moscow rather than to the local population.

A Russian-speaking American who traveled across the Soviet Union at this time claimed that in Leningrad, Kiev, and Moscow, there was talk—quiet talk—of revolution. The idea might have been fanciful, but over ninety years ago, Lenin and Trotsky were instrumental in overthrowing the czar and creating the USSR.

The political reality of the time was—that Gorbachev's overtures was nothing more than the latest manifestation of Soviet deception and that the withdrawal scenariowas really the maturation of the grand scheme to seize Afghanistan. The temporary passivity of the world will be manipulated, support for the resistance will be condemned, discord will be sown, and the mujahideen alliance will become a fiasco. The offensives will escalate while nonengaged forces withdraw, and when finally all Soviet troops have left, a Marxist "coalition" will emerge from the ashes. And if ever another resistance begins, a phone call will be made and the Red Army will return to Afghanistan, this time permanently. Maybe the Afghan SSR will one day loom over India and the Persian Gulf.

Such deception would not be unprecedented. In January 1986, Gorbachev declared that in the interest of peace and good will, the Red Army would partially withdraw from Afghanistan. Six regiments were brought home. And another six regiments were simultaneously sent in. It was a routine, wholesale replacement, and it probably somehow advertised the Soviet posture in the war. A large percentage of the original invading forces were Central Asians. They were available nearby, and Kremlin masterminds hoped that their racial, cultural, linguistic, and religious affiliations with the Afghans would help win the resistance over to Communism. When the Central Asians instead began defecting with their weapons and training, Moscow recalled almost all of them, replacing them with Slavs. By 1986, Slavs, too, were misbehaving. Scores had deserted. Perhaps hundreds, at one time or another, refused to fight, even risking execution or life in a Siberian gulag for insubordination. War can drive men to such extremes. Maybe the six regiments replaced were incorrigible. Or maybe they had simply finished their tours of duty.

The world has rightly predicted that the Soviets will widraw and the war will end, and Afghanistan will belong to the Afghans and to Islam. And the prediction became a reality after the USSR has lost. It was also predicted that the Afghan leadership and the free world will force the Soviets to accept the consequence of war, and its leaders will be forced to accept the consequences. If *perestroika* succeeds, the Communist common market embraces the world market, China is modernized, and East and West at last remember the enemy that brought them together—the world domination goals of the Nazis—perhaps the imperialism will end, and global cooperation and enlightened technology can begin. The loss of Afghanistan won't be so bitter, and the establishment of an independent, nonaligned, and neutral Islamic government in Kabul won't seem like such a threat.

At was also predicted that, the greatest obstacle to peace was not the stalemate in Geneva (Diego Cordovez is continuing mediation between Islamabad and Kabul). The stalemate can be resolved, and neither Pakistan nor the United States (in secret negotiations with the Soviet Union) will forsake their efforts to foil the survival of the Communist regime.

The greatest obstacle, ironically, was disagreement among the resistance. At that, the most important juncture in Afghanistan's history since Ahmad Shah Baba returned from Persia and declared the independence of his homeland, the mujahideen were endangering their own prospects for the future of their nation. The monarchy was gone, secular republicanism wasgone, and thesoon Communism was defeated. If sound wisdom and sober foresight prevail, the Afghans can at last define and establish an Islamic democracy; not a Western democracy, but a way of government founded on the equality envisioned by Muhammad the Prophet

But for many influential mujahideen, wisdom does not prevail.

Early in March,1989 the seven organization leaders assembled in a private conference to appoint the executive interim council. Engineer Ahmad Shah, an American-educated, very spiritual man, who joined the resistance in 1980, served as vice president of Etihad. He was unanimously nominated as chief of the interim government. But a few days later, one leader, Sibghatullah Mujadidi of the National Liberation Front, changed his mind.

Mujadidi, in regular contact with Zahir Shah and frequently visiting him at his villa in Rome, Italy, alternately opposed and favored restoring the deposed king to power to serve as a figurehead, beneath which the faction-ridden society could reunite. Mujadidi's inconsistency was baffling, and his reversal was especially untimely.

During a 1981 press conference in Peshawar, Gulbuddin Hekmatyar said, "Zahir fertilized the ground and sowed the seeds of Communism in Afghanistan's Muslim society." During an interview with a BBC (British network) correspondent, Abdul Rasul Sayyaf said, "Zahir opened the doors, Daoud invited them in, and Taraki and Babrak sold the country to the Russians." Burhanuddin Rabbani and Yunis Khalis nurtured similar sentiments, but Sayed Ahmad Gailani is withheld his opinion. However, Moulavi Mohammad Nabi Muhammad, leader of

Harakat-i-Inqelab-i-Islami, have supported Mujadidi proposal, which would lend dangerous cogency.

Meanwhile, Mujadidi, rather than exercising patience and trying to understand that the anti-Zahir leaders were simply eager to protect the future of Afghanistan by averting the impetuous restoration of despotism, unrestrainedly accused his colleagues of "dictatorial tendencies" and publicly compared them to the Soviets and Najibullah. More drastically, Mujadidi threatened to quit the alliance, although he abandoned the idea.

If Kabul is, in fact, attempting to sow discord, Mujadidi's recent deliberations are abetting it. If discord succeeds and no interim government is agreed upon, peace could once again steal away. Unless the resistance can stand united and provide an uncontested government to replace Najibullah's regime, Kabul may continue to prolong the withdrawal, asserting that "interparty feuding" might carry over to national politics. The real hazard would be an ambivalent government's vulnerability to subversive Communist agents.

The world has become too dangerous a place for anything but cooperation.

Energy should not be devoured by strife but rather in solving more paramount controversies—most importantly, the composition of the *loya jirga*, or grand council, that will appoint the post-withdrawal leadership.

I extend my recommendations: nine representatives from the refugee population, three representatives from each of the seven mujahideen organizations, and twenty-nine representatives from inside Afghanistan—one from each province—should be elected to appoint the interim government.

Each representative should be elected by the inhabitants or members of his own category, and no one from another category should interfere with or attempt to influence the voting. Ideally, those elected will be elders, religious or political leaders, and scholars/intellectuals. Each should be profoundly anti-Communist, with some accreditation in the resistance.

Each representative should have equal voice. The assembly should convene for several days and the final decision should be at least marginally acceptable to all parties. For instance, the Zahir issue should perhaps be buried, as a less controversial figure may be just as effective in office, if not more so. Zahir was, after all, never very capable, and in his old age, he is certainly not qualified to tackle the enormous task of reconstruction. Also, any inclination to accept Moscow's and Kabul's proposal for a coalition should probably be shunned. Neither the Communists nor the non-Communists could be trusted to win in such a situation. Even if the Communists didn't engage in intrigue, they would eventually be shot by one of the millions of non-Communists whose homes were bombed and whose families were killed.

It must be remembered by all voting Afghans that the personal convictions of the interim appointees are only peripherally important. If fortitude, dedication, and certain selflessness are sought, the liability of military rule or dictatorship will be averted. And when Afghanistan is rebuilt and becomes secure and at peace, then national elections may take place. Our one and a half million martyrs will have died for something.

The future promises incredible challenges.

Our children have grown up in the sophisticated West, or in the introverted refugee camps, or in the war. Twenty thousand have been educated in the USSR.

Our men and women have ingested war and horror. Our beloved land is desolate.

But we are Afghans, descended from millennia of such challenges. Together, we will fare well, *Insha-Allah*.

May the next generation behold the fertile ground, prosperity, and technological success. Afghanistan should modernize, perhaps even pursue a space program. Men of Islam once charted the night skies, and they, as all men, should travel to the stars and see the earth as Allah Almighty sees it. ***May they see a world where men live free.***

CPSIA information can be obtained at www.ICGtesting.com
Printed in the USA
BVOW01s1336110914

366142BV00001BC/49/P